Early Language Learning: A Model for Success

A volume in
Contemporary Language Learning

Series Editor: Terry A. Osborn
University of Connecticut

Early Language Learning: A Model for Success

by
Carol M. Saunders Semonsky
Marcia A. Spielberger

INFORMATION AGE
PUBLISHING

80 Mason Street • Greenwich, Connecticut 06830 • www.infoagepub.com

Library of Congress Cataloging-in-Publication Data

Saunders Semonsky, Carol M.
  Early language learning : a model for success / by Carol M. Saunders Semonsky, Marcia A. Spielberger.
      p. cm.
  Includes bibliographical references.
  ISBN 1-59311-082-0 (pbk.) — ISBN 1-59311-083-9 (hardcover)
  1. Language and languages—Study and teaching (Elementary)—Georgia.
I. Spielberger, Marcia A. II. Title.
P57.U7S28 2004
372.65'044—dc22

                                                              2004011543

Copyright © 2004 Information Age Publishing Inc.

All rights reserved. No part of this publication may be reproduced, stored in a retrieval system, or transmitted, in any form or by any means, electronic, mechanical, photocopying, microfilming, recording or otherwise, without written permission from the publisher.

Printed in the United States of America

CONTENTS

List of Tables and Figures	vii
Acknowledgments	ix
Introduction	xi
1. Creating and Implementing the Georgia Elementary School Foreign Languages Model Program	1
2. From Theory to Practice	17
3. The Curriculum	41
4. Program and Student Assessment	69
5. Conclusion	101
References	107
Appendix A. Original Application Form	113
Appendix B. The Georgia Elementary School Foreign Languages Model Program Original Fifteen Sites	117
Appendix C. Approximate Budget for Beginning an Elementary Foreign Language Program with 15 Teachers	119
Appendix D. Philosophy and Pedagogy	121
Appendix E. Third Grade Web Theme All About Me: Language Structures, Progress Indicators, Vocabulary, Objectives and Assessment Recommendations	123
Appendix F. Joe Frank Uriz's Unit Plan	131

Appendix G. Joe Frank Uriz's Assignments and Grading Rubrics ... 143

Appendix H. Student Oral Proficiency Assessment (SOPA) Rating Scale ... 149

Appendix I. Student Attitude and Ability Questionnaire ... 155

Appendix J. Georgia Elementary School Foreign Languages Model Program Brochure, 2002-2003 ... 157

LIST OF TABLES AND FIGURES

Figure 3.1.	Thematic Web for Third Grade	43
Figure 3.2.	Joe's Content-related Web	52
Table 2.1.	Grade Level Articulation for Theme of Family	33
Table 3.1.	How National Standards for Foreign Language Learning Are Addressed in the Quality Core Curriculum	47
Table 3.2.	Joe's Broad Language Objectives and Overarching Assessment Activities	54
Table 3.3.	Unit Outline for *I Can Take Care of a Pet*	56
Table 4.1.	Combined Percentages of Model Program Third Grade Students in Seven Schools According to Listening Comprehension and Oral Fluency on the SOPA Rating Scale in 1997	72
Table 4.2.	Comparison in Percentages of Third and Fifth Grade Model Program Students in Listening Comprehension on the SOPA Rating Scale in 1998	74
Table 4.3.	Comparison in Percentages of Third and Fifth Grade Model Program Students in Oral Fluency on the SOPA Rating Scale in 998	74
Table 4.4.	Comparison in Percentages of Model Program and Non-Model Program Fifth Grade Students in Listening Comprehension on the SOPA Rating Scale in 1998	75
Table 4.5.	Comparison in Percentages of Model Program and Non-Model Program Fifth Grade Students in Oral Fluency on the SOPA Rating Scale in 1998	75
Table 4.6.	Percentages by Level for SOPA Ratings of Third Grade Model Program Students in 2001	77
Table 4.7.	Percentages by Level for SOPA Ratings of Fifth Grade Model Program Students in 2001	79
Table 4.8.	Means and Standard Deviations of SOPA Ratings for Oral Fluency and Listening Comprehension for Third Grade Students in the Model Program and a Traditional FLES Program	80
Table 4.9.	Means and Standard Deviations of SOPA Ratings for Oral Fluency and Listening Comprehension for Fifth Grade Students in the Model Program and a Traditional FLES Program	80
Table 4.10.	Statistical Analysis of FL and Non-FL Student Performance on the ITBS	88
Table 4.11.	Math-Related Progress Indicators from the Model Program Curriculum	89
Table 4.12.	Reading-Related Progress Indicators from the Model Program Curriculum	89
Table 4.13.	Responses to Student Attitude and Ability Questionnaire	93
Table 4.14.	Ranking of Weighted Questionnaire Responses for All Languages	97
Table 5.1.	2001-2002 Demographics of Model Program Schools by Percents	104

ACKNOWLEDGMENTS

It takes many people working together to create and maintain a quality program such as the Georgia Elementary School Foreign Languages Model Program. We would like to thank those people who have played important roles in its development and implementation. We wish to recognize current and former members of the Georgia Department of Education, Greg Duncan, Horst Bussiek and Werner Rogers for their vision for Georgia's children and especially the current foreign language specialist at the Georgia DOE, Elizabeth Webb. We would like to thank the members of the Georgia General Assembly for their continued support of the program and former Lieutenant Governor Pierre Howard for shepherding the initial program through the legislature. We would also like to thank Carol Ann Pesola Dahlberg, Helena Curtain and other experts in the field for their contributions in program development, teacher training and observation and curriculum writing. We would like to express our appreciation to the researchers at the Center for Applied Linguistics, Carolyn Adger, Beverly Boyson, Donna Christian, Nancy Rhodes and Lynn Thompson for conducting research about the Program and for granting us permission to cite their research in this book. We would like to extend our gratitude to Joe Frank Uriz for allowing us to include his excellent unit plan and other materials as an example of effective implementation of the Model Program curriculum. To the Model Program teachers and students, you have been an inspiration to us and to anyone who observes you. We would also like to thank the parents and other advocates for the program, in particular members of the Georgia Coalition on Language Learning and the Foreign Language Association of Georgia for their ongoing support of elementary foreign language study.

We would also like to acknowledge our respective colleagues at Georgia State University and Fulton County Schools for their support of our project. Last but certainly not least, we owe a deep debt of gratitude to our families and friends for their understanding and support of this endeavor.

INTRODUCTION

During the mid and late 1980s, as research became more and more convincing that early second language learning would produce the most student success in terms of language proficiency, a long term goal of the foreign language office of the Georgia Department of Education was the creation of an elementary foreign language program. The ideas for this creation began and were developed in detail over a period of about five years. Today Georgia is fortunate to have one of the top rated elementary school foreign language programs in the nation, the Georgia Elementary School Foreign Languages Model Program (Model Program). Both of us have played a significant role in the continuing success of the program. Marcia A. Spielberger was the Georgia Foreign Language Supervisor who coordinated the program from 1992 to 1999 and Carol M. Saunders Semonsky conducted extensive research on the program as well as trained and assessed its teachers. Through our experience, we have learned about a wide variety of elementary foreign language programs in the United States and recognize that the Georgia Elementary School Foreign Languages Model Program represents best practices in elementary foreign language education.

Our aim is to provide a detailed description of the process of initiating, maintaining and assessing a top quality elementary foreign language program and to assist planners by providing them with a model for a workable program. Another goal is to describe the challenges we have encountered so other program developers can avoid similar pitfalls. The primary audience for this book is policy makers, state and district level educators, including supervisors who have responsibility for foreign languages, principals, teachers and foreign language educators who are interested in best practices in elementary foreign language education or who wish to begin a high quality elementary foreign language program at the state or district level. We hope that by relating our experiences in Georgia we can provide a useful guide for program development.

Chapter 1 explains the inception and initial planning of the Georgia Elementary School Foreign Languages Model Program. Chapter 2 will provide a history and a summary description of elementary foreign language program designs. It will show how the Model Program is based on second language acquisition theory and represents best practices in elementary foreign language education. Chapter 3 describes the Model Program curriculum and provides an example of how to use the curriculum to plan a unit of instruction. Chapter 4 describes program and student assessment. Chapter 5 concludes with successes and challenges.

One of the most exciting parts of writing this book has been to look back and track the actual origins of the program and to see and reflect on the incredible progress that has been made. This program has evolved in a state that 20 years ago had almost no foreign language being taught at the elementary level to one that at the time of this publication not only has approximately 14,000 students in the Model Program, but thousands of others in elementary programs that have begun and developed as a result of the Model Program. It is such an amazing feat that today Georgia has become the state cited with the status of being best in the nation in terms of what the Model Program's elementary students know and are able to do in a foreign language! It is quite an accomplishment for which many of us in Georgia can be proud.

CHAPTER 1

CREATING AND IMPLEMENTING THE GEORGIA ELEMENTARY SCHOOL FOREIGN LANGUAGES MODEL PROGRAM

INCEPTION

In Georgia, during the 1960s and 1970s, there were elementary school foreign language programs offered in some school districts. As was the case in many parts of the country, when funding diminished for these loosely connected programs, the programs disappeared. This meant that in Georgia for at least a decade there were few elementary school foreign language offerings. During the 1980s, it became known through research that those who begin their second language study at a young age and who continue their study over a long sequence are more successful second language learners (Krashen, Stephen, Robin, Scarcella, & Long, 1982). Greg Duncan, as Foreign Language Coordinator at the Georgia Department of Education during the late 1980s and early 1990s, had a vision that Georgia needed to begin an elementary school foreign language program. He recognized that there was an increasing body of evidence in favor of the benefits of an early start to language learning. In 1988, he organized a small group of foreign language educators to participate in the K-8 Foreign Language Methodology Course. The idea was to begin a "Training the Trainers" design that would continue on if the program progressed. The training was provided by nationally known experts in the field, including Carol Ann Pesola Dahlberg and Myriam Met. The participants spent their mornings learning theory about second language acquisition of young children and methods of teaching them and spent the afternoons actually working with groups of children. This was truly an eye-opening and rewarding experience for those who participated. The course was very successful in convincing a variety of foreign language professionals that an early start in second language learning is the best way to ensure the success of the learners.

Having garnered the support needed from within the profession, the foreign language staff at the Georgia Department of Education began the process of designing a program for the public schools. They ultimately decided that Georgia should create and develop an elementary school foreign language program that was sequential and substantive. The plan was to begin in a number of school districts around the state, with the initial schools serving as models for others to follow. The original plan was to begin with 60 programs around the state, but in order to reduce the cost and thus improve the chances of funding, the number of programs was later reduced to 45. Ultimately, in the spring of 1991, after several annual rejections by the state legislature and with encouragement from the Georgia Department of Education, Georgia decision makers took a small risk of $361,000, enough to fund a kindergarten foreign language program in 15 school districts across the state. The negotiation for this funding was purely political and involved some "horse-trading" among lawmakers that included trading "blueberries for French." The funding was secured by the lieutenant governor, a francophile himself. While much of the last minute negotiations of the budget were done privately and details of these negotiations were not known, it was made public that the lieutenant governor agreed to support special funding for blueberry production in exchange for others to include a small foreign language program in the state budget.

Model Program vs. Pilot Program

Why has the program been called the Georgia Elementary School Foreign Languages Model Program? The original rationale that still holds today is that the program serves as a *demonstration* model on which others can base their programs. Many educators, lawmakers and others have often referred to the program as a pilot. We and others who have been closely involved with the program have refused to call it such because the word pilot in education circles implies that a program is being tried out to determine whether or not it is successful. At the end of the trial period, the pilot ends. The only way in which we could accept the word pilot is by using one of its meanings from the dictionary that means *guide*. We gladly accept that the Model Program serves as a *guide* or *model* for others to follow. The original goal has always been to expand, not to eliminate, the Model Program in more schools throughout the state.

IMPLEMENTATION

Initial Steps

Immediately after the funding was approved, the foreign language staff at the Georgia Department of Education began formulating an implementation plan. Three nationally known experts in the field of early language learning, Helena Curtain, Carol Ann Pesola Dahlberg, and Myriam Met, contributed ideas for the implementation plan. It included developing criteria for the program and spelled out the responsibilities and commitments at the state, system and school level. The implementation also addressed requirements for teachers, curriculum development, a schedule for staff development and provisions for foreign language staff at the Georgia Department of Education to do frequent teacher observations.

While those at the Georgia Department of Education knew that if a program could be started, it would gain the support of local educators and community members, it was imperative that informing educators and educating the general public about early foreign language learning be a part of the implementation process. Therefore the foreign language staff at the Georgia Department of Education held a one day conference in the late spring of 1991 to which school personnel who might be interested in participating in the new program were invited. More than 100 attendees from across the state came to get details on the what, when, where, why and how of this new program. The rationale for students to have an early start in foreign language instruction, the research of successful language acquisition in young children and research about improved SAT scores for students with longer sequences of foreign language instruction were all presented.

4 The Georgia Elementary School Foreign Language Model Program

Application Process

The conference attendees received a copy of the guidelines and application packets for participating in the Georgia Elementary School Foreign Languages Model Program. The original guidelines for school systems making application to the Georgia Department of Education for the Model Program were stated as follows. Systems must:

1. Agree to follow the Foreign Languages in the Elementary School (FLES) curriculum model which is a sequential program of language learning leading toward student proficiency in the target language;

2. Agree to follow the kindergarten foreign language curriculum guidelines available from the Georgia Department of Education (1st, 2nd, 3rd, and 4th grade guides would be available in the following years);

3. During the first year, agree to provide foreign language instruction to all kindergarten students in the selected site(s). During Year 2, the program would become K-1; Year 3, K-2; Year 4, K-3; Year 5, K-4 (provided the Georgia Legislature continued program funding). The FLES teacher may provide instruction for a maximum of eight 30-minute class periods per day. Two smaller schools may share the FLES teacher. The number of students per class period cannot exceed state standards;

4. Agree to provide foreign language instruction for a minimum of 30 minutes daily for every kindergarten student during Year 1 and in grades 1-4 as the program continues;

5. Employ a teacher who meets one or more of the following criteria:

    a. Possesses a K-12 certificate in the selected foreign language;
    b. Possesses a 7-12 certificate in the selected foreign language and is willing to complete the K-8 foreign language methods course before commencing the second year of the program;
    c. Is a native speaker of the selected foreign language and possesses a K-4 (early childhood) certificate and is willing to complete the K-8 foreign language methods course before commencing the second year of the program;

6. Agree to pay the salary difference between the state allocation for the teacher and the local system's allocation for that teacher;

7. Ensure that the foreign language teacher will attend all designated in-service training programs as provided by the Georgia Department of Education;
8. Be willing to commit its support to the program for a five-year period of time provided the state legislature continues to fund the program;
9. Provide letters of support for the program's introduction into the elementary school;
10. Submit no more than one application per system (Georgia Department of Education, Curriculum Services, 1991).

In awarding of grants, preference was given to schools that did not offer a FLES program in grades K-4 at that time.

It was decided that there would be a total of 15 programs across the state, one for each of the ten congressional districts that existed at that time, and five at-large programs to be selected from the five additional best applications. One reason for the decision to award programs by congressional district was the many calls received early in the implementation stages by Marcia A. Spielberger, Foreign Language Consultant at the Georgia Department of Education at that time. Personnel in small rural districts asked if it was worth their taking the time to apply for the program or if all of the programs were automatically going to be awarded to the large metropolitan Atlanta districts. These questions convinced Georgia Department of Education staff that they needed to ensure equity when distributing the programs. Since the Georgia Board of Education has one member for each congressional district, it was decided that the Model Program would be created with the same kind of balanced representation and would thereby provide equal opportunity for access to small rural districts. This actually gave some school systems an advantage because in some cases only two or three school systems within a congressional district applied. It is important to other school systems and states that wish to initiate a program to consider a competitive application process by providing opportunities, like the one described above, that encourage small districts to apply.

The application form, a copy of which is located in Appendix A, included an agreement to comply with the program criteria, a description of the school community, examples of the specific ways the district could provide additional support for an elementary school foreign language program, its transience rate, how the system would integrate and promote the program in the community, a description of future articulation into middle and high school, willingness of the system to serve as a demonstration site and its choice of language. Districts were asked to select their top three choices of language on the application. It was explained to districts at the conference that not all programs would be funded for Spanish language instruction and they were encouraged to consider other languages.

When all of the applications were received, there were more than 50 for the 15 available programs. They were sorted into ten different congressional districts for evaluation. A group of neutral readers was selected by the Georgia Department of Education foreign language staff to read the applications. The readers included members of the general education community, foreign language educators who did not participate in the competition and others who were knowledgeable in the field of early foreign language instruction. The readers rated each application according to the criteria that had been set. The best application was selected for each of the ten congressional districts throughout Georgia and the other five were selected based on their strength on an at-large basis. Once the selections were finalized and approved by the Georgia Department of Education, selected schools from 15 school districts were invited to participate in the Georgia Elementary School Foreign Languages Model Program. A list of these schools and districts can be found in Appendix B. While many districts did select Spanish as their first choice of language, others chose French, German or Japanese. Of the original 15 language programs, eight districts offered Spanish, three offered French, two offered German and two offered Japanese. The districts were notified and began interviewing in June of 1991 in order to find qualified teachers to begin the program that August.

Over the last ten years, there have been two additional opportunities for local districts to apply to participate in the Model Program. When some districts were either unwilling or unable to follow the criteria, they dropped out of the Model Program and other districts applied and replaced them in 1997. There was also a reapplication process in 2000 which included existing systems and new systems because the Georgia Board of Education wanted to ensure that other systems had an opportunity to apply for the Model Program. As of the 2003-2004 school year, there are 26 schools representing 15 systems participating in the Model Program. As a result of the strengths and positive results of the Model Program, a number of districts have replicated the design with local funding.

A Setback and a Revival

In early summer of 1991, due to a state budget crisis, all new funding, including the allocation designated for the Georgia Elementary School Foreign Languages Model Program, was cut from the budget. Even though the school districts had already been selected and implementation plans were in place, the Georgia Department of Education was obliged to cancel all plans for implementation, including the hiring of teachers. It may be of interest to some local school district personnel to know that several districts who had already hired teachers and had made plans for implementation began their programs in 1991 with no state support. As a result, these districts were always one grade level ahead of the Model Program sites. It was a difficult situation at the Georgia Department of Education in the summer of 1991 because the foreign language staff had finally succeeded in getting a program funded and almost immediately lost it.

In the spring of 1992, Lieutenant Governor Pierre Howard was successful once again in securing funding. The program and all plans to implement it were revived, and this time it began successfully. The 25 schools within the 15 original districts that had been selected to participate were invited to restart their plans from the previous year. All facets of the program remained the same, including hiring teachers who met the criteria. One challenge that some local systems encountered was that they had experienced unusual growth during the 1991-1992 school year and needed additional personnel. As part of the original agreement, the local system was committed to having the foreign language teacher, who was funded partially by the state, teach a maximum of eight classes per day. If there were more than eight classes, it was the local system's responsibility to fund additional personnel for the extra classes. This was done by sharing teachers from middle and high schools for a portion of the day or by hiring part time teachers.

CHARACTERISTICS OF THE MODEL PROGRAM

Essential Components

There are certain characteristics that stand out about the Model Program that lead to its effectiveness. It has a commitment to long, articulated sequences beginning in kindergarten and extending throughout elementary school, with the aim of articulation into middle and high school. It delivers 30 minutes of foreign language instruction to every student on a daily basis throughout elementary school. It is expected that teachers will teach exclusively in the target language and that learners will use the target language to express themselves. Teachers are expected to hold or work toward P-12 foreign language certification. Teachers address all four language skills, integrating them with culture. There is integration of both national and state foreign language standards. The curriculum format uses thematic webs where the focus for each major theme is modified and expanded with each successive grade level of the program to include developmentally appropriate topics. The curriculum is spiraled and articulated from year to year with continual student progress along a continuum toward proficiency. The curriculum includes content-related topics reinforcing the regular school curriculum. There is a competitive application process for school districts to participate in the program, thereby ensuring that districts who want the program and who are willing to abide by the program guidelines participate in the Model Program. The program encourages involvement of parents and the school community. Intensive professional development is provided by experts in the field of elementary school foreign language methodology. Participating school districts agree to release Model Program teachers to participate in the professional development sessions and to allow them to conduct cross-site observations. There is ongoing teacher and student assessment.

Teacher Qualifications

In order to maintain the integrity of the program, the Georgia Department of Education was obliged to insist that all local systems strictly adhere to the criteria that were set. The original criteria included hiring qualified foreign language teachers who were certified to teach P-12 or who had 7-12 certification and were willing to convert their certificates. It was around this time that Georgia required all new foreign language teachers to be P-12 certified. Another option was to hire native speakers of the selected language who were certified elementary teachers. After some years of experience, we recognized that native speakers who were elementary school teachers needed specialized training. For districts who wish to begin early foreign language programs, if native speakers with elementary school certification are hired to teach in a FLES program, they must be provided with additional training in second language acquisition. A teacher who is trained in his native language as an elementary school teacher will no doubt have the skills to teach and interact with young school children, but will not have a background in second language acquisition and methodology. Those teachers with 7-12 certification have most likely not had any exposure to theories of how young children acquire language and may use teaching methods that are not appropriate in the elementary school classroom. While teacher certification differs from one state to another, the practice of providing additional training in second language learning for those without full licensure in elementary school foreign language teaching is imperative if a top quality program is to be maintained. One of the strengths of the Model Program is its ongoing, practical training in the methodology of teaching foreign languages to young children. In the application, local systems made commitments that they would release teachers both to attend staff development sessions and to observe teachers in other systems. They also committed to provide the foreign language teacher with his or her own classroom. If that were not possible, they were to provide a rolling cart for the teacher to use in moving from class to class, a workspace and a storage area within the school.

Scheduling and Articulation

The Georgia Department of Education, after consultation with experts, decided to offer foreign language instruction 30 minutes per day, five days per week. The Model Program began foreign language with kindergarten instruction in the fall of 1992. The initial plan was to begin with kindergarten and to add the next grade each subsequent year, i.e., first grade during the second year, second grade during the third year and so forth. This same pattern continued until all programs offered a kindergarten through fifth grade sequence. All students, including those with special needs, in the grade levels within the schools participating in the Model Program received daily instruction in the selected foreign language.

While the program is well articulated in kindergarten through fifth grade, the articulation is a challenge when students move from elementary schools to middle schools and from middle schools to high schools. In order to be successful with regard to articulation, we recommend that systems or states collaborate with the principals, assistant principals and persons who are responsible for curriculum in the schools at all levels. When these administrators play an active role in the entire process from the beginning, they are more likely to support the program over time. Since education personnel change frequently, it is important for the Model Program supervisors to involve new school personnel as soon as possible after hiring. Another challenge is that in middle school students from the Model Program schools should not be blended with students from non-Model Program schools. This presents a scheduling problem for middle schools and in some cases, requires that small classes be scheduled so that the Model Program students can continue in a separate, articulated track. This can become a funding issue.

Initially, some school level administrators may regard eight 30-minute classes as a light teaching load. They must be convinced and educated about the program in order to understand the demands of effectively teaching an elementary foreign language class. It takes a high level of physical energy on the part of the teacher to teach in the target language and to implement the eight to ten different activities usually occurring during one 30-minute class. Furthermore, most foreign language teachers teach more than one grade level and come in contact with 150 to 200 students each day. The foreign language teachers need extra planning time to write lesson plans using the curriculum which is not textbook based. They also need extra time to prepare activities and materials in order to scaffold their language. Teachers must create most of the materials themselves. The reality is that these elementary foreign language teachers are itinerant, meaning that they go from classroom to classroom using a cart. The cart functions as a desk, file cabinet, holder of supplies and materials and sometimes functions as a white board and chart holder. Given all of these factors, an eight-class load is not unrealistic.

At the inception of the Model Program, some districts selected one large school to participate while others chose two smaller schools to be shared by one teacher. Those wishing to start programs should be aware that one large school with eight classes can be managed by one teacher. In the case of two small schools, administrators should be encouraged to assign fewer general duties to that teacher or to allow the teacher to instruct only a total of seven classes since travel between two schools must be done on a daily basis. The travel takes valuable teaching and planning time and requires that the itinerant teacher be familiar with the events and administration of two schools.

FUNDING COMPONENTS

There are several key funding components of the Georgia Elementary School Foreign Languages Model Program that are essential to its success. They are: teacher salary and benefits, professional development, curriculum development and enhancement, materials and supplies, and assessment development. In order to create and maintain a successful elementary foreign language program, all of the components must be present and effective. The best analogy to describe how essential these components are is to compare them to the ingredients in baking a cake. If one or more ingredients is omitted or used in an incorrect quantity, such as using only half of the flour required in a cake recipe, a well-formed, delicious cake will not be the result. It must be clear to all parties that the five components mentioned above are absolutely necessary, not optional. Since readers of this book may be interested in beginning a program in the near future, we have included in Appendix C an approximate budget for beginning an elementary foreign language program with 15 teachers. While some of the figures are estimates, the budget can serve as a guide for someone who wishes to build a program from the beginning.

Teacher Salaries and Benefits

The financial commitment on the part of the local district to participate in the Georgia Elementary School Foreign Languages Model Program was to pay the difference in salary and benefits between the state award and the local salary and benefits for each teacher in the Model Program. In the Georgia Model Program, the base beginning state salary for a teacher with a Bachelor's Degree in 1992 was the amount that the state funded to the individual districts. That figure was $21,740. While teacher salaries in Georgia have risen considerably in the last decade, the state funded portion to the district at the time of this printing is $25,651. The local districts provide the rest of the salary for each teacher, which for some urban and suburban districts with large local supplements is more than 50% of the total salary, while in small rural districts, there is no supplement added. All districts must provide benefits that must be calculated at a rate of 30% of the salary figure. Since teacher salaries differ from one district and one state to another, these calculations will vary on an individual basis.

In cases where additional teachers were needed to provide instruction to all students in the grades taught, it was the responsibility of the local system to provide funds for these additional personnel. The commitment by the district to the program was to continue its support as long as the state funded the Georgia Elementary School Foreign Languages Model Program. In the first year of the Model Program, each system was allotted one teacher, while in the second year, each system was allotted two teachers. After that time, as different systems experienced varied amounts of growth, the Georgia Department of Education allotted teachers based on the enrollment of the participating schools. One teacher slot was awarded for every eight classes to be taught.

Professional Development

The professional development at the outset of the program consisted of a five-day workshop in the summer and 3 or 4 two-day workshops during the academic year. All Model Program teachers were required to attend. As the program grew, only new teachers were asked to attend the summer seminar. All Model Program teachers are now expected to attend one weekend retreat in the fall and the Foreign Language Association of Georgia annual conference in the winter. In various years of the Model Program, some funds were set aside for specific summer training for all new teachers. In some cases where teachers have needed to improve their second language proficiency, they were partially funded for a language immersion program for teachers either in the United States or abroad. If teachers needed additional methodology training, they were offered a partial scholarship to attend intensive workshops. While the Georgia Department of Education budgets funds to pay for the tracher trainers and workshops, teachers are usually required to pay a portion of these professional development sessions in order to ensure their commitment to the Model Program. In different years of the Model Program, varying amounts of funding have been available for professional development.

One facet of the Model Program that has contributed to its strength is the relationship built among Model Program teachers. This relationship, while not quantifiable, has contributed to the success of the Model Program in part because of the opportunities for Model Program teachers to share their techniques and successes with one another. Many times at workshops, the enthusiasm of various presenters generates a kind of synergy among participants and there is an energy that results from the sharing of new ideas.

Curriculum Development and Enhancement

It was noted in the criteria that the curriculum to be developed by the Georgia Department of Education would be developmentally appropriate, sequential in nature and would tie in closely with the regular curriculum. While the development of the curriculum will be discussed in detail in Chapter 3, it first began when the kindergarten curriculum was drafted by a small group of teachers and Department of Education administrators during the summer prior to the beginning of the program. In the summer of 1993, and in each subsequent year, a draft curriculum was written for the new grade and the draft curriculum that had been used during the previous year was revised so that it might better reflect what could and would be taught. This process repeated itself over a number of years. We regard the curriculum as *a living document* that can be changed as needed. The fact that there was funding for the curriculum revision and that there continued to be teachers interested in and capable of revising the curriculum has contributed to the success of the Model Program. In terms of cost, teachers are paid a flat fee of approximately $100 per day for curriculum drafting and revision as well as travel expenses when necessary. The number of teachers needed is dependent on where in the cycle the revision is. For example, the first and second drafts require more writers than the later revisions. Additionally when the generic curriculum is drafted, the writers should represent a cross section of languages, but when specific language components are written, there must be at least two writers per language.

Materials and Supplies

At the outset of the Model Program, an amount of $500 per teacher was provided by the Georgia Department of Education. This funding was included in a separate line item for materials and supplies in the contract between the Georgia Department of Education and each school district. This amount was later increased to $1,000, but then decreased as the number of teachers grew. Since textbooks are infrequently used in the Model Program, the materials and supplies to develop teacher-made materials are essential to the success of the program. Making materials is an important component of the summer and weekend workshops. More experienced teachers bring materials that they have found effective for implementing particular units to share. In addition, Model Program teachers organize a "Make and Take" session annually at the Foreign Language Association of Georgia's winter conference and at some weekend meetings. The Georgia Department of Education funds these sessions.

Assessment

In the very early years of the Model Program, the focus of Georgia Department of Education foreign language staff was on hiring appropriately trained teachers, staff development and curriculum development. In 1995, during Year 3 of the Program, the Georgia Department of Education requested that researchers from the Center for Applied Linguistics (CAL) in Washington, D.C. perform a program evaluation of the Model Program. CAL found the program to be very effective and especially praised the strength of the staff development component. The other three assessments measured the language proficiency of students in various grade levels. The result of each was extremely positive and various details of the evaluations will be explained in Chapter 4. It is crucial to the success and continuation of any program that it be assessed from the outset. In terms of cost, each contract with the Center for Applied Linguistics was different and ranged from $10,000 to $49,000.

CHALLENGES

Funding

The original funding for the Georgia Elementary School Foreign Languages Model Program was a line item of $361,000 in the annual state education budget. When the first year of the program was complete, the funding for kindergarten went into the "continuation budget" of the Georgia Department of Education. Only the funding for the subsequent grade, first grade, was "new" funding and was placed in a line item in the annual state budget of new funds. The fact that new funding, though it was not a large amount, was a line item each year made it very noticeable and vulnerable. The foreign language leaders in the state have been able to negotiate successfully for that small addition every year up to the present time and were able to maintain the continuation portion. Once the program was funded in kindergarten through fifth grade, the total budget was more than $2,000,000 and that budget item was large enough to be noticed and has remained vulnerable.

The long range plan of the Georgia Department of Education foreign language staff was that there eventually be a funding formula by which any Georgia school or school district that met the criteria for the Model Program could receive the funding. With changes in leadership at the state level, this never became a reality and each year that a new grade level of the Model Program was funded was time for a celebration. The implementation of a funding formula continues to be a goal of advocates of the Georgia Elementary School Foreign Languages Model Program. At the time of this printing, foreign language educators and advocates continue to work with the Georgia Office of Planning and Budget and other state officials to devise a plan for future funding that is within the realm of possibility. It is our hope that eventually any school or school district that meets the criteria established for the Model Program will receive some monies from the state. The balance of the funding would be provided by the district. We recommend to districts or states that are beginning a program that a percentage of funding be supported by the district because it is a way for a local school system to demonstrate its real commitment to the program.

Budget Cycles

The Georgia General Assembly usually ends it annual session in late March or early April. This timeline is an annual challenge for both state and district administrators because by springtime, local school district budgets for the following year are in their final stages of preparation and it is difficult to adjust them. We suggest that when planning a new elementary foreign language program, this incongruence of funding cycles regarding decisions about the budget at state and district levels be avoided if possible.

Enforcement of the Criteria

When the contracts between the state and the individual school districts were first written, they included language that stated that the district must meet the criteria set forth in the original guidelines. After several years, personnel in various districts changed and were unaware of these specific criteria. It was necessary for the Georgia Department of Education foreign language specialist to include very specific guidelines that must be met as part of the contract between the Department of Education and each district. By being very explicit, districts were held accountable for all details of administering the program. The one criterion with which schools had the most difficulty was the adherence to the maximum foreign language teacher class load of eight classes per day. In order to ensure quality teaching and to avoid teacher burnout, administrators in local systems must insist upon the eight-class limit.

Maintaining Continuity for Program Success

The Model Program funding was initially shepherded by Pierre Howard when he was Lieutenant Governor. When he no longer held that position, the supporters of the program were forced to seek new advocates. In some cases, while certain legislators were willing to support the program, they were not willing to be the standard bearers. Additionally in the political arena, the players change frequently. Whenever possible, those interested in starting and maintaining an elementary foreign language program should seek a broad base of support from a variety of educators, community members, parents, business and government leaders across the state in order to guarantee that the funding for the program continues.

One important lesson we learned was that the program could not depend on any one person for its success. The program must have many strengths and numerous participants and supporters. Several different foreign language specialists at the Georgia Department of Education have overseen the Model Program in various years. The third State School Superintendent to have the Model Program as part of the Georgia Department of Education's successes was sworn in during January of 2003. Neither a state, nor district nor school can be dependent on one administrator or teacher for the success of the program. Administrators and teachers, like many other citizens, are transient and do not always remain in one position or in one location.

It has been a continuous challenge on the part of local systems to advocate for the Model Program and to ensure its funding. A variety of advocacy approaches has been used, including but not limited to a press conference at the Georgia Capitol to announce the success of assessments of the Model Program, performances by students at the Capitol and at the Georgia Board of Education, numerous letters written to decision makers by educators, parents and students and visits with legislators and budget officers.

CONCLUSION

We are both proud of the roles we have played in the implementation and maintenance of the Georgia Elementary School Foreign Languages Model Program. Our purpose in writing this book is to share the successes and the challenges we have met along the way and to provide practical guidance to others who wish to begin an elementary school foreign language program in their states or school district. We have been honest in telling the story of the Model Program, how it started, the stumbling blocks we have encountered and the wonderful feelings we have experienced when the successes of the program have been made public. In the subsequent chapters, we will explain the research, the curriculum and the assessment in detail so that the information can be used to apply to different situations in other parts of the United States or abroad. It is our hope that our book can serve as a kind of road map along the way to building successful FLES programs.

CHAPTER 2

FROM THEORY TO PRACTICE

INTRODUCTION

When the Georgia Department of Education Curriculum Services staff designed the Model Program they wanted to be sure that they selected a design based on accepted theory and one that best addressed the needs of Georgia students. To accomplish this task, the planners took into consideration historical theories, methodologies and existing program designs with the intent of creating a successful elementary school foreign language program while avoiding mistakes of the past. Chapter 2 shows how the Georgia Elementary School Foreign Languages Model Program is grounded in theory and exemplifies best practices in elementary school foreign language education. The first part of this chapter describes selected germane theories of psychology and second language acquisition and gives an historical overview of elementary school foreign language methodologies. The rationale for a content-related curriculum is set out. The next part of the chapter describes various types of elementary school foreign language program designs. The chapter continues with a discussion of how the Model Program exemplifies both the theories discussed and best practices of foreign language education.

Early Language Learning: A Model for Success, 17–39
Copyright © 2004 by Information Age Publishing
All rights of reproduction in any form reserved.

HISTORICAL PERSPECTIVES

Early Theory and FLES Methodology

Foreign language methodology historically has had close ties with psychological theories of learning. Early FLES was closely aligned with behaviorism, and modern FLES models rely on constructs of cognitive psychology. We will begin by examining early FLES design and its ties to behaviorism. The psychologist, B. F. Skinner, laid out his theory of operant conditioning in 1938 in his book, *The Behavior of Organisms*, hypothesizing that learning occurs when the consequences of an action are either positively or negatively reinforced. In 1957, Skinner applied these theories to language learning in his book, *Verbal Behavior* (Skinner, 1957). According to Skinner, languages are learned as a result of habit formation which comes about by repetition and reinforcement. After enough repetitions of a structure, the structure becomes automatic (conditioned). If the speaker uses appropriate language he is rewarded by a positive response, such as comprehension on the part of the interlocutor or approval by the teacher, which, in turn, increases the likelihood that the language will be repeated (learned). In the late 1950s, foreign language teachers applied these behaviorist theories to language learning methodology, specifically, the Audio-Lingual Method (ALM). The main techniques of ALM were memorization and rote repetition, and activities such as substitution drills, chain drills and pattern-response became the focus of classroom instruction, all reinforced by intensive use of the language lab. The students would typically memorize a dialogue. The teacher would then begin structure practice by having students repeat a sentence based on the dialogue several times. When students had memorized this sentence, the teacher would give a stimulus for a slight modification or transformation such as a change from one subject to another, from singular to plural, from affirmative to negative and the like. The students would repeat the new structure until they could repeat it without hesitation. The new structure was then considered learned. The Audio-Lingual Method emphasized speaking and listening over reading and writing, although these skills were included to a lesser degree. The method had high expectations, promising to produce fluent speakers of the foreign language.

The emphasis on memorization, repetition and habit formation characteristic of ALM is illustrated by the following description of a Level 1 FLES program in French. The learning sequences included:

1. Practicing correct pronunciation and intonation;
2. Listening to, memorizing and reproducing dialogues and other speech patterns;

3. Speaking in choral groups;
4. Repeating exercises and drills of basic language structures;
5. Reading and copying materials that have been mastered orally;
6. Acquiring cultural appreciation as an integral part of language learning;
7. Learning gestures that are a part of the language and culture (O'Rourke and the California State Department of Education, 1967).

Behaviorism, with its dependence on external stimuli and extrinsic rewards, failed to take into account the individual factors learners bring to their own learning process. Factors such as motivation, attitude, effort, attention, personality and different learning styles were largely ignored by the behaviorists. By its very name, ALM emphasized aural/oral learning at the expense of the visual, kinesthetic learning that is so important for most young learners. It is not surprising that the original FLES programs were short-lived. Such techniques as memorization and drill hold little interest for young children, and such methodology runs contrary to the current view that children learn best by acquiring a foreign language in meaningful situations. Several researchers reported on the demise of the early FLES movement (Alkonis & Brophy, 1961; Stern, 1963). The two most important reasons for the collapse of ALM were that, contrary to claims made by educators, students in an ALM program did not become fluent in their foreign language and the program was very expensive to maintain. After paying for intensive teacher training in the technique, for elaborate language labs and for expensive materials, the federal government as well as local districts were no longer willing to spend their money on a program that did not work as promised. Curtain and Pesola (1994) detailed further reasons why early FLES failed: a lack of qualified teachers, insufficient program planning, a lack of articulation, lack of appropriate materials, and, as they so well put it, "the tedium and irrelevance of the audio-lingual method" (p. 19). Page (1966) indicated that a major problem with audio-lingual FLES was the failure of most programs to adapt teaching techniques to the cognitive development of the students they served.

In the 1970s, many school districts eliminated FLES altogether, allocating their funds for other areas. The teaching of foreign languages in the elementary school, while not as widespread, continued but did not have a fixed or generally accepted program model. Some districts continued with the ALM method while others initiated immersion or partial immersion programs or took an eclectic approach. Schinke-Llano (1985) referred to foreign language learning in the 1970s as "a decade of inactivity" (p. 2).

In 1979, the need for foreign language study again came to the forefront for political reasons. President Jimmy Carter appointed a Commission of Foreign Language and International Studies. The commission's report, *Strength through wisdom: A Critique of U.S. capability. A Report to the President from the President's Commission on Foreign Language and International Studies* (1979), pointed out the urgent need for foreign language study in an increasingly international and interdependent world. Other works, such as former Senator Paul Simon's (1980) *The Tongue-tied American* and D.P. Gardner's (1983) report, *A Nation at Risk*, echoed the need for language study. These reports galvanized the American foreign language community into action. However, unlike with the implementation of earlier FLES based on a single program design and methodology, educators now had the choice of a variety of program designs. They could coordinate their specific language learning objectives, available funds, and teacher resources with a design of their choice. They could choose from a variety of immersion programs, requiring the most amount of time, resources, and training, but providing the greatest language fluency, to several new FLES designs, requiring a lesser investment of resources and having the tandem goal of language proficiency and content reinforcement, to foreign language exploratory requiring the least amount of time and emphasizing an introduction to the language and cultures rather than language proficiency itself.

Later Theory and FLES Methodology

New movements and theories of second language teaching appeared. The American Council on the Teaching of Foreign Languages (ACTFL) established its proficiency guidelines in the 1980s. These provided a descriptive evaluation of what kinds of language students should be able to produce as they advanced in their language learning. The Proficiency Guidelines described the language functions and discourse types learners should control, with what degree of accuracy and under what circumstances or contexts for each of four levels: Novice, Intermediate, Advanced and Superior. Global assessment of production skills replaced the discrete item assessment of structure knowledge as was emphasized in grammar-translation and ALM methodologies. By clearly delineating learner production characteristics, for instance that paragraph-level discourse does not appear until learners reach the Advanced Level, the ACTFL Proficiency Guidelines have prevented the unrealistic expectation of fluency in a short time promised by the ALM proponents.

Cognitive psychology, with its emphasis on the active role of the learner, influenced second language acquisition theory. The cognitive psychologist, David Ausubel (1968), objected to the behaviorist model of rote memorization because it was too fragmented. It was similar to dumping out a puzzle but not putting the pieces together into a whole. Ausubel contended that learning is like putting the puzzle together. It is a continuous process in which new pieces of information are attached to existing knowledge so that a new, meaningful whole, like the completed puzzle, is formed. Ausubel (1968) referred to this phenomenon as "subsuming." Brown (1993), in his discussion of Ausubel, elaborated on meaningful learning. He said, "Any learning situation can be meaningful if (1) learners have a meaningful learning set—that is, a disposition to relate the new learning task to what they already know; and (2) the learning task itself is potentially meaningful to the learners—that is, relatable to the learners' structure of knowledge" (p. 81). Commonly used teaching techniques, such as accessing background knowledge, developing meaningful cognitive sets, and using advanced organizers, as well as concentration on individual student learning styles and strategies originate from Ausubel's assumptions.

McLaughlin, Rossman, and McCloud (1983) related Ausubel's subsuming theory to second language acquisition, referring to "restructuring" as an important aspect of second language acquisition. They described a process of second language learning that was on a continuum from controlled to automatic. Controlled processing occurs when language skills are first introduced and practiced but are not yet permanent parts of the student's foreign language production. Automatic processing occurs when the student has practiced the skill enough and has had an opportunity to relate it to what he already knows. He "restructures" the skill into a usable form that he can readily access. If we return to our metaphor of the puzzle, when the language restructuring occurs, it is similar to finally fitting the puzzle piece in the correct spot. McLaughlin's Information Processing Model had a second dimension, that of focal or peripheral attention, depending on the degree of overt attention required to perform a skill. McLaughlin believed that children learn a second language by paying peripheral attention, focusing more on the meaning and nature of the task than on the language rules needed to perform it. Adults, on the other hand, tend to move from controlled processing and focused attention to automatic processing and peripheral attention as they learn their foreign language.

Both Ausubel's and McLaughlin's models have implications for foreign language teaching in the elementary school. The development of meaningful cognitive sets and of relating new knowledge to previous experience provide an important rationale for the use of content to teach children. If a content topic has been introduced in the regular classroom, when the foreign language teacher addresses the same topic, the students may find it easier to fit the piece into their mental puzzle. The secondary treatment in the foreign language class will serve only to broaden the students' cognitive set related to the topic. The content-related curriculum also centers the children's attention on meaningful tasks rather than on the parsed-out language structures found in many adult classes. Young learners can focus on the task at hand, such as predicting if objects will sink or float, rather than on the language itself. Conversely, if the students are introduced to a concept in the foreign language classroom, they will have the beginnings of a cognitive set that they can access when the same topic is taught by their regular classroom teacher. If the concept is, for example, estimating length, in the regular math class the students can estimate in inches using English, and in the foreign language class they can estimate the length in centimeters using their foreign language. Both class treatments serve to reinforce the students' concept of estimation of length and have the further advantage of broadening the concept of multiple systems of measurement. Students reap a double benefit in the foreign language class by increasing their proficiency in both math and their foreign language. The ideas of another language theorist, Cummins, supported the idea of the mutual benefit of content and language. He hypothesized one broad area of linguistic and cognitive knowledge and offered what was referred to as the "Think Tank" model (Cummins, 1981). He contended that underlying the use of the native and the second language is one integrated source of thought and that all language contributes to the growth of this Think Tank (Baker, 1988).

That children learn languages differently from adults, with mostly peripheral attention, also has implications for the elementary school classroom. Because adults use focal attention and are cognitively able to analyze abstract rules, it may be appropriate to teach them *about* the language. But it is generally not appropriate for young children. While both children and adults should be taught *in* the foreign language using strategies that center on meaningful use of the language, adults may benefit or even prefer rule-focused instruction, but children should be engaged in activities that hold their interest and are appropriate for both their cognitive level and their language level.

A second model of second language acquisition greatly influenced foreign language teaching in the 1980s and 1990s. It was the Input Hypothesis developed by Stephen Krashen (1981). The basics of the theory are presented here; their application to the program design used by the Model Program will be presented in the next section. Krashen's theory has five basic hypotheses:

Hypothesis 1. Comprehensible Input. Krashen maintained that the first component of foreign language learning was exposure to the foreign language itself. He referred to this as input. Krashen said that exposure alone was insufficient to learn a language; otherwise, we could simply travel to the target language country, turn on the television or radio and become fluent. The input must be the right kind of exposure, what Krashen called "comprehensible input" (p. 21). In order for input to be comprehensible, it must be tailor-made for the learners, so to speak. Krashen said that the input should be approximately one level above the learners' current level of language knowledge. Krashen described this optimum level of input as input + 1 or $i + 1$. Although, according to Krashen, not all input must be at *exactly* the $i + 1$ level; students exposed to a combination of $i + 1$, $i + 2$, and $i + 3$ could still learn, but not at, for example, $i + 9$ or $i + 10$.

Hypothesis 2. Affective Filter. This hypothesis said that just because the teacher provides $i + 1$, it does not necessarily follow that the input is received by the learners. There are certain affective variables that can interfere with the input being received. Krashen called this barrier to input the affective filter. It works along the following lines: if a student is motivated to learn the language and is at ease with the learning situation, his affective filter is down and the comprehensible input can get through. If, on the other hand, the student is unmotivated or the learning environment makes him anxious or nervous, the affective filter will go up, preventing the input from being attended to by the learner.

Hypothesis 3. Natural Order. In this hypothesis Krashen took into consideration the fact that certain grammatical structures seem to be learned in a predictable order. Language acquisition, no matter what the method used, occurs in a preordained progression. This was reminiscent of Chomsky's (1965) theory that humans have a biologically determined capacity for language located in what he called the "language acquisition device."

Hypothesis 4. Acquisition versus Learning. This hypothesis stated that learners developed language skills in two different ways: they could *acquire* the language through a process that is subconscious or they could *learn* language skills through the conscious application of the rules of grammar. Children, Krashen said, gained language proficiency through the acquisition process in a natural way that was similar to the way they acquired their first language. Krashen contended that true language competency was based on acquired, not learned, language.

Hypothesis 5. Monitor. Krashen believed that *learned* language was edited language, and he theorized an editing device that he called the monitor. Monitoring, or the conscious analysis of linguistic rules, interferes with language proficiency. It adds an extra step, a mental checking-for-correctness process, that hinders language output. It is analogous to using spell check on a computer for each sentence before going on to the next sentence. Krashen believed that there was an "optimal use" of the monitor (1987, p. 19). This was the case of the adult learner who had a sense of what language structures to monitor and which to let go.

McLaughlin and Krashen are only two of many theorists who developed various models of second language acquisition. Other theories include those of Asher (1986), Bialystok (1978), Ellis (1986), and Tarone (1988). In 1991, Larsen-Freeman and Long found more than 40 theories of second language acquisition. It is clear that there is no one generally accepted theory or methodology of foreign language learning. Furthermore, each theory raises questions. How can we tell what $i + 1$ is? How does a teacher provide instruction at the $i + 1$ level for a classroom with 25 students, each at a slightly different stage of learning? What is the "Natural Order" of structures for different languages? Why can there be no crossover of learning and acquisition? Isn't monitoring/learning good if the learners are adults? Is input sufficient for learning to occur or does the learner apply effort and learning strategies to augment his own learning? Must we have controlled processing before automatic? How do focal and peripheral attention fluctuate? How do controlled and automatic processing interact? What effect does student attitude and motivation play in language learning? Because of the complex and indefinable nature of language learning that occurs within the brain of each learner and that is affected by so many variables, it is unlikely that linguists will ever be able to come up with the one correct theory of first language or second language acquisition. Yet, each theory sheds light on the process.

In the pages to follow, we will link many of these theories with the classroom practices of Model Program teachers.

ELEMENTARY SCHOOL FOREIGN LANGUAGE PROGRAM DESIGNS

When the Georgia Elementary School Foreign Languages Model Program was initiated there were a variety of elementary school program designs already in existence. Designs differ in their goals of the amount of foreign language proficiency they can reasonably expect students to achieve and in the resource commitments needed to meet these goals. Rhodes, Tucker, and Clark (1981) described three main types of programs available in the early 1980s.

The first program design was Foreign Language Experience (FLEX). FLEX does not have language fluency goals nor is it the start of an articulated sequence of language learning. It is a form of enrichment that can be taught by someone with a minimal background in foreign languages, and it is designed to help students decide which language to study at a later time (p. 9). Typically, students study, mainly in English, aspects of the culture and geography of the countries where the foreign language is spoken. They may be exposed to small bits of the foreign language such as numbers, colors, some food, clothing, school items, etc. Very often the lone foreign language teacher, who speaks only one target language, is required to teach two to five different language introductions during the course of a FLEX experience. FLEX programs require the least amount of time and financial investment but also deliver the least amount of language. In many respects they are just as similar to social studies classes as they are to foreign language classes.

The second program design was immersion in its various degrees: total immersion, early immersion, late immersion, delayed immersion, partial immersion and two-way immersion (Genessee, 1984; Rhodes et al., 1981). In most immersion programs, the content area teacher **is** the language teacher or vice versa since some or all of the regular elementary school course curricula are taught in the foreign language. Immersion has the highest language and content goals accompanied by the greatest investment in time and resources.

The third main category Rhodes et al. (1981) identified was FLES, but they were very careful to distinguish it from its predecessor of the 1960s. They divided FLES into two categories: "revitalized FLES" and "curriculum-integrated" foreign language. They described revitalized FLES programs as follows:

They have classes up to five days a week either before, during or after school. They are called 'revitalized' because they take a different approach than the traditional programs of the 1950s and 1960s. Unlike traditional programs that were not aimed at development of communication skills, revitalized FLES programs emphasize conversational skills as well as cultural awareness. These programs vary in their specific goals and in the amount of time spent per day in the classroom (p. 8).

The last program design mentioned in the Rhodes et al. study was that of curriculum-integrated foreign languages. Curriculum-integrated foreign language programs have a daily language class that is conducted in the language, and an additional language and culture component taught by the regular classroom teacher.

Another new program design to enter the elementary school foreign language arena in the 1990s was that of content-related instruction. Several researchers (Arnall, 1992; Curtain, 1993) pointed out the difference between a content-*based* foreign language curriculum such as immersion, in which the foreign language teacher is responsible for teaching the content objectives, and content-*related* instruction in which the foreign language teacher reviews and reinforces content objectives taught in the regular classroom, but is not the only teacher responsible for the mastery of the cognitive concepts. Foreign language educators have made a case for content-related FLES programs. Curtain and Pesola (1994) pointed out that in a FLES program which is limited to 30 minutes a day or less, it is not realistic for the foreign language teacher to actually do "effective initial teaching of increasingly sophisticated and abstract ideas" (p. 151). This does not mean, however, that the foreign language class cannot include content-related activities. According to Curtain and Pesola, "Through theme-based, integrative teaching, however, the foreign language class can reenter and reinforce important concepts from mathematics, social studies, and other areas, drawing from earlier grade levels as well as from grade-level-appropriate curriculum" (Ibid.). Heining-Boynton (1991) described the benefits of a content-related foreign language program. She listed four benefits: (1) the content provides a "meaningful vehicle" (p. 64) for foreign language use; (2) the content-related foreign language class provides review and reinforcement of concepts learned in the regular classroom; (3) content-related FLES encourages such higher order thinking skills as analysis, synthesis and evaluation; and (4) content-related programs create "positive public relations that justify early foreign language instruction in what is felt to be an already-crowded elementary curriculum" (Ibid.).

In presenting a rationale for content-related instruction, Louton and Louton (1992) provided an hypothesis as to what differences exist between learning in first and second languages. They called this the Language Acquisition Gap (LAG) hypothesis. They explained that rote memory, one of the mainstays of ALM, can allow for symbol substitution such as *hunt* or *chien* for the word dog. However, when dealing with connotative elements such as meanings, emotional experiences and physical associations, internalized symbols and schemata add a dimension that simple symbol substitution of rote memory cannot address. According to Louton and Louton:

> During the regular classroom instruction the teacher, working toward concept development in the native language, calls upon the full range of the students' experiences and comprehension. In the foreign language class, however, the language symbols are 'new' to the nervous system which provides little on which the students can hang these new symbols. This results in acquisition of the foreign language with its meaning and concepts lagging behind the native or primary language and concept, a language acquisition gap (pp. 4-5).

One reason why ALM ultimately failed as a comprehensive teaching methodology may be that it focused too much on symbol substitution and did not touch on "sensori-motor elements and basic images" (Ibid., p. 5). While Louton and Louton admitted that there have been strides in recent FLES methodology, they believed that the gap between first and second language acquisition must be addressed in the classroom. They contended that a content-related curriculum, rather than a content-based curriculum was appropriate for most FLES programs. They suggested that learning about the language should be incidental and that the main focus of a foreign language class should be "the acquisition of new learning in various subject areas by capitalizing on the pupils' innate curiosity which originates from the sensori-motor stage" (Ibid.). They likened the relationship of subject content and foreign language to a moving train, with the content representing the train "on which the foreign language can be loaded and the train and the cargo become one" (Ibid.).

What are the implications of a content-related approach for methodology? In keeping with the LAG hypothesis, the initial concept should be introduced in the regular classroom and then reviewed and reinforced in the foreign language class. It is a kind of logical progression. The regular classroom teacher introduces a concept from one of the content areas, for example, the solar system, community workers, division, or character traits. The foreign language teacher then recycles the concept to teach the foreign language; while practicing the language, the students reinforce and broaden their grasp of the concept, which, in turn, should help their performance in the regular classroom. It is in this way that language and content are mutually reinforcing. While language and content tend to be more synchronous in early grades, with a growing divergence in later grades, this does not mean that content-related instruction cannot be incorporated. It does mean that the language will have to be more intensively scaffolded and that the tasks required of the learners must fit their language ability. The content can still serve as a meaningful base upon which language tasks can be constructed.

THEORY IN ACTION

The above discussion of elementary school methodology and second language acquisition theory as it relates to young children highlights some of the factors taken into consideration when the Model Program was developed. In keeping with tenets of cognitive psychology, the Model Program emphasizes meaningful use of the language and de-emphasizes grammatical analysis and rote vocabulary use. Vocabulary is presented in meaningful thematic contexts with teachers using techniques such as vocabulary webs instead of foreign language/English lists. This lack of overt attention to structure study reflects McLaughlin's view that children learn languages through automatic, not controlled processes and Krashen's view that children acquire language without the use of monitoring. In other words, children in the Model Program do not learn the language structures first and then use them to create meaning. Instead, they use the language in meaningful, content-related or story-form contexts in which grammar is learned only as a function of its necessity to meaningful exchanges.

The Model Program curriculum designers consciously incorporated topics from the grade-appropriate regular elementary school curriculum. This relates to Ausubel's concept of background knowledge as well as to McLaughlin's belief that children learn best through peripheral attention. For example, in a unit on the solar system in a third-grade foreign language class, the students will call upon their knowledge of the solar system garnered in their English language science class. The solar system vocabulary in the foreign language will be easier for the students to understand if they already have concepts such as the rotation of the planets around the sun and on their axes, or the planets' distances from the sun, set in their minds from their science class. They can access this background knowledge to help them make sense of the foreign language vocabulary without resorting to an English translation. Conversely, the projects they do in the foreign language class, such as mobiles of the solar system or descriptive booklets of the planets' characteristics, will only serve to reinforce scientific concepts common across all languages. In addition, while the children are making their planet, sun, stars or comet hats to wear for a reenactment of the rotation of the planets around the sun, the language structures receive only peripheral attention while the task at hand receives focused attention. McLaughlin would describe this process as automatic processing with peripheral attention. Krashen would classify this as acquiring the language rather than learning it.

The Model Program teachers apply several other aspects of Krashen's Input Hypothesis. First, teachers, in accordance with Krashen's Comprehensible Input Hypothesis, have several responsibilities to their students. Teachers must use the target language for instruction without translating into English in a manner so as to make it comprehensible to the students. Presumably, they will not use the same level of vocabulary or sophistication of structures in a kindergarten language class as in a third grade class. Model Program teachers modify their speech much the same way adults adjust their speech when speaking to their own children. Curtain and Pesola (1994) list the various names of this modification, "motherese," "teacherese," "caretaker speech," or "foreigner talk." Some of the characteristics of teacher talk they give are (1) a somewhat slower rate of speech; (2) more distinct pronunciation; (3) shorter, less complex sentences; (4) more rephrasing and repetition; (5) more frequent meaning checks; (6) use of gesture and visual reinforcement; (7) greater use of concrete referents; and (8) scaffolding (pp. 56-57). The Model Program teachers make frequent use of extra-linguistic support, such as gestures, pictures, objects and realia, as an aid in making the input comprehensible. All of these techniques used by teachers to make the language comprehensible to the students fall under the general term of scaffolding. Second, in accordance with the Affective Filter Hypothesis, the teachers seek ways to motivate the students and make them excited about learning the foreign language. The teachers also create a classroom atmosphere that is conducive to language learning; that is, free from anxiety, embarrassment and threat. The language class is fun and contains activities that are appropriate both for the language abilities of the learners and for their cognitive level. Third, to promote language acquisition as opposed to language learning, the teachers present the language in a natural context rather than teaching explicit language rules. Fourth, in order to avoid the use of too much monitoring, the teachers are forgiving of imperfect language output and know that errors are a natural part of both first and second language learning.

The Model Program teachers developed what was originally called the *Statements of Understanding* and are now referred to as the *Model Program Philosophy* (Georgia State Department of Education, Curriculum Services, 2002a). Many of these commitments exemplify Krashen's hypotheses. The complete Philosophy statements are located in Appendix D. Below are some of them in more detail:

As a Georgia Elementary School Foreign Languages Model Program teacher, I demonstrate support for the philosophy of the program when I:

1. Teach 98-100% of the time in the target language;
2. Avoid using translation as a tool for clarifying meaning;
3. Provide learners with a rich, target language environment that includes extended listening opportunities, such as narration, descriptions and explanations;
4. Use the target language for classroom management as well as for instruction;
5. Present vocabulary in chunks and in context rather than as isolated words or lists;
6. Plan and teach around a theme;
7. Seek to integrate concepts from the general elementary school curriculum in every lesson and every unit;
8. Provide learners with meaningful concrete experiences, making extensive use of visuals, props, realia, and hands-on activities;
9. Use songs and rhymes to reinforce meaning and practice language.

The first five commitment statements focus on the dedication of the teachers to provide comprehensible input in the foreign language. Model Program teachers use the foreign language in natural contexts, such as narration, description and classroom management. They do not present vocabulary by means of lists to be memorized, but in contextualized chunks.

What provides the context for the natural acquisition of the language? As indicated in commitment statements 6 and 7, the teachers use thematic planning and integration of content-area concepts. The content-related curriculum helps teachers tailor their foreign language class to Krashen's $i + 1$ level. What the teachers plan for their foreign language students is compatible with the students' ages and cognitive abilities at each grade level. For instance, in mathematics, the Model Program has more complex objectives for grade 3 than it does for kindergarten. For example, one of the kindergarten objectives is "Students will solve simple mathematical problems dealing with addition using numbers 0-10" (Georgia State Department of Education, Curriculum Services, 2002b). But by third grade a comparable objective is, "Students will estimate and measure length of selected objects using the metric system" (Ibid.). The concepts of estimation and the metric system would not be comprehensible to kindergarten students, even in English, because these concepts are not cognitively appropriate for that age group.

One of the benefits of the content-related, spiraled curriculum that the Model Program uses is that it helps teachers focus on the topics and vocabulary appropriate to present to their students in the foreign language at each grade level. It is this precise indication in the Model Program curriculum of both contexts and language that enables the teachers to approximate Krashen's $i + 1$ and to teach in the target language without frustrating their students.

Commitment statements 8 and 9 have to do with Krashen's affective filter. The teachers strive to make the foreign language class fun and comfortable for their students, in Krashen's terms, to keep the affective filter low. They do this by planning high-interest thematic lessons that incorporate a variety of activities appealing to different learning styles and preferences. They also use techniques such as games, songs, stories, and rhymes that are fun for the students and at the same time reinforce language and content skills.

HOW THE MODEL PROGRAM EXEMPLIFIES EFFECTIVE ELEMENTARY SCHOOL FOREIGN LANGUAGE PROGRAM DESIGN

We have seen how the Model Program bases itself on good methodology and theories of learning and second language acquisition. When formulating the Model Program, the designers also strove to be a model of best practices in elementary school foreign language learning. They took into consideration the recommendations for elementary school foreign language program design as described by the national association of foreign language teachers, the American Council on the Teaching of Foreign Languages (ACTFL). In 1991, ACTFL defined the characteristics of effective foreign language programs for young learners. Curtain (1993) describes the 12 characteristics:

1. Access and equity.
2. Program design choice.
3. Extended sequence.
4. Articulation.
5. Systematic curriculum development and assessment.
6. Instruction appropriate to the developmental level of the students.
7. Appropriate materials, rich in authentic culture and language and related to the curriculum.
8. Evaluation both of student achievement and of program success.

9. Staffing by teachers who are certified in elementary methodology and whose language skills are at least at the advanced level of proficiency as rated by ACTFL's Oral Proficiency Interview.
10. Continuing professional development.
11. School and community support.
12. Cultural awareness and understanding are explicit goals of the program.

We shall now examine in detail how the ACTFL characteristics of a successful FLES program relate to the Model Program. Each characteristic will be discussed separately.

1. Access and equity. The program should be available to all students. Research indicates that FLES should not be restricted to high achieving students, but that students of below-average intelligence also profit from early language study (Garfinkel & Tabor, 1991; Tabor, 1987). To this end, the Georgia program is all inclusive; that is, **all** students in the grades receiving the foreign language participate in the program without regard to intelligence or achievement level. When evaluating applications by new systems, the Model Program review panels seek to provide access to diverse learners: urban, suburban and rural. At this time, due to limited funding, not every elementary school child in Georgia receives foreign language instruction. Ideally, this would be the case. The Model Program, as opposed to a pilot program which is tried and then eliminated if not successful, was designed to serve as a model of excellence in foreign language education upon which districts desiring to offer top quality instruction could base their program. Every school district in any part of Georgia has had at least three opportunities to apply for the program. The intention initially was that, eventually, funding would be available to all schools that meet the criteria. To date, this has not happened, although the idea is still being considered. Several districts have funded expanded elementary school foreign language instruction based on the Model Program design, and their teachers have been invited to participate in in-service development designed for and facilitated by Model Program teachers. Additionally, other schools and districts have the opportunity to observe and collaborate with Model Program schools that serve as demonstration sites. Currently, Georgia has "the best program for as many as possible" rather than "a less effective program for all."

2. Program design choice. While FLEX, FLES and immersion are program designs that Georgia elementary schools can choose to offer, the Model Program is a FLES program with a content-related component.

The curriculum is relatively fixed, but individual participating districts can choose to offer a language of their choice.

3. **Extended sequence.** Foreign languages should be available from kindergarten through twelfth grade. While all Georgia high schools and many middle schools offer foreign languages, there is currently no operational articulated extended sequence for grades K-12. The first students who participated in the Model Program are currently in the eleventh grade. While most districts are still struggling with the complex issue of continuing the foreign language into the middle school, where only a portion of the students will have been exposed to the foreign language K-5, several districts are currently working on such middle school articulation. The *Georgia Quality Core Curriculum* (2002b) describes such an articulated sequence reflecting the desire that more and more districts provide the 13-year sequence. Funding issues and teacher availability make this a continuing challenge.

4. **Articulation. There should be coordination of program objectives throughout the extended sequence.** The Model Program makes a conscious effort to spiral and recycle the progress indicators and objectives from year to year. The progress indicators for the theme of family for grades K-3 located in Table 2.1 illustrate how the language is recycled. As stated before, the kindergarten children get a limited introduction to the

Table 2.1. Grade Level Articulation for Theme of Family

Grade	Topic Theme	Progress Indicators
Kindergarten	Meet My Family	K.4. Students will produce basic information about selected family members:
First	Look at My Family Pictures	1.1. Students will identify and name family members and describe their physical characteristics.
Second	We're Going to a Family Reunion	2.1. Students will recognize and produce extended family member names. 2.2. Students will use names, qualities, and descriptors to give information about family members and peers. 2.3. Students will use emotional descriptors and feelings to describe family, self and peers.
Third	Family Members Help Each Other	3.1. Students will identify household responsibilities of various family members.
Fourth	Family Sitcom Family Puppet Show	Fourth grade progress indicators for family have not been written.
Fifth	The Family in Fairy Tales	5.5. Students will describe personal attributes of family members

Source: Georgia Department of Education, Department of Curriculum Services (2002b).

topic, but by recycling the theme and enlarging upon it from year to year, students can gradually talk about the topic in more depth. The tasks progress from simple identification in kindergarten and first grade, to description in second and third grade, to creating an original story in fifth grade. The language objectives found in the curriculum also are recycled from year to year. They begin with more basic statements in kindergarten and are added to or modified as the children progress through the program. For instance, kindergarten children "listen to stories for enjoyment" but in later years, students "read for enjoyment" (Georgia Department of Education, Curriculum Services, 2002b).

5. **Systematic curriculum development and assessment.** The Model Program teachers in conjunction with experts in the field of elementary school foreign language education write and revise the curriculum on a regular basis. At first, the curriculum was drafted and piloted for a year before it was adopted for general use. Teachers using the draft curriculum provided feedback as to how the curriculum should be revised in order to improve its quality in subsequent years. This process was repeated as additional grade levels were added during the progressive implementation schedule. In 1998, a group of Model Program teachers and other experts transformed the Model Program curriculum into the Georgia *Quality Core Curriculum* (QCC) for Foreign Languages, K-5. In other words, the Model Program curriculum became the statewide elementary school foreign language curriculum. It is reviewed and revised in accordance with regular updating of the curriculum by the Georgia Department of Education. The important factor is that the stakeholders, i.e., the teachers themselves, participate in the systematic revision of the curriculum they will be teaching.

6. **Instruction appropriate to the developmental level of the students.** Effective foreign language instruction derives from several factors: appropriate subject content and thematic contexts, appropriate foreign language vocabulary, structures and functions, and correct techniques and pacing for presenting them to the students. It has already been stated that the Model Program curriculum is based on grade-level appropriate content-related topics. By consulting the academic subject area curriculum guides, the foreign language curriculum writers were careful to align their topics with what is cognitively appropriate for each age group. Also previously discussed is the way the vocabulary builds upon itself from year to year. Vocabulary and language structures are carefully chosen to complement the lesson content and the language level of the students. The curriculum also helps teachers pace their lessons. Kindergarten teachers know that they can spend shorter amounts of time with a lot of practice and repetition on each topic, while fourth grade

teachers know they can do more in-depth activities after recycling language presented in earlier grades.

The final component of appropriate instruction is the use of suitable techniques to present the language and content. In this regard, Model Program teachers take into consideration both developmental psychology and second language acquisition theory. Piaget (1963) described four stages of cognitive development for children. Children in kindergarten and first grade are in Piaget's preoperational thought state. They are governed by perception rather than by logical thought. These children are egocentric in the sense that they cannot conceive of a world beyond that of their immediate experience and they can deal with single classes, not subclasses nested within larger groupings (Lefrancois, 1982). The Model Program's main curriculum theme, *The World of the Child*, allows the students to talk about familiar experiences. The kindergarten and first-grade teachers use many manipulatives in their teaching that appeal to the children's senses. Children are encouraged to hear, touch, smell, taste and see the actual objects they are using in their foreign language. Students in grades 2-5 are in Piaget's concrete operational stage. They can classify in nested groups, size, shape and color, for example, and rank objects in different orders. They also have the ability to manipulate numbers. The Model Program curriculum continues to focus on concrete concepts incorporating the use of objects and manipulatives in grades 2-5, but more advanced concepts are also treated. Students begin graphing and sorting; they not only name and recognize numbers, they begin to use them to calculate, measure and estimate.

Kieran Egan (1979) described layers of educational development. According to Egan, children from ages 4/5 to 9/10 are in the mythic layer. Children in this layer view the world in terms of absolute categories without seeing the subtle gray areas in between. They can focus on binary opposites such as good/bad, happy/sad, etc., and they interpret the world from within. The use of story form to present concepts in a logical order with a beginning, middle and end is important. Around the age of 9, children move into the romantic layer. They develop an idea of the world outside themselves and they try to interpret this world. They are fascinated with detail and like extremes. They like heroes who succeed against a threatening and alien world. Model Program teachers, taking a cue from Egan's ideas, use story form to present concepts. For example, one Model Program teacher used a book he purchased in France, *Bon Appétit, Monsieur Lapin* (Boujon, 1985), to introduce the color and texture of foods. Many other teachers make their own big books or "smush books" to create a story around a topic. Teachers, using the curriculum, begin in kindergarten and first grade with a direct focus on the child's immediate world, but by fourth and fifth grade the focus shifts to a wider interpretation of the world. For instance, while treating the thematic topic of *My Community,* the kindergarten subtheme, *Can You Help Me?* stays close to home by exposing the young children to the names of a few selected community helpers. By fourth grade, the subtheme is *How Communities Differ,* and the focus shifts to a comparison of the child's own community with a community in a target culture.

   7. **Appropriate materials, rich in authentic culture and language and related to the curriculum.** The Model Program provides a certain amount of funding for teachers to buy materials. The original group of 15 teachers received a stipend of $1,000 for acquisition of materials. As the number of teachers increased each year, the amount for materials has varied from as little as $100 to as much as $1,000 per teacher, based on the availability of funds. Individual districts, schools and PTA organizations also provide varying amounts of additional funds for materials. Curtain and Pesola (1994) stressed the importance of materials. They said the materials "provide the means for creating the concrete context that is so necessary for meaningful communication" (p. 283). They continued,

> Because children require hands-on learning experiences with concrete objects, the foreign language classroom must have a wide variety of objects and materials available—as many of them as possible from the target culture. Such materials offer a richness and texture not available even in the most carefully designed textbook. This need for a wide range of materials is one of the most marked differences between teaching elementary and middle school children and older students (p. 283).

Model Program teachers make and buy many manipulatives and materials. Some materials they use, although the list is by no means complete, are: puppets, objects for sorting, hoops for making Venn diagrams, plastic foods, musical instruments, pocket charts, community helper hats, styrofoam balls to make mockups of the solar system, live plants, stuffed animals, real foods, musical tapes, posters, large maps, shower curtain floor plans, colorforms, balls, plastic dinosaurs, masks, books and many other items. During in-service and pre-service training, teachers are asked to create activities from simple materials such as paper plates, plastic spoons, and paper lunch bags. They are asked to purchase an item for less than $5 from a store that does not cater to educators, such as Wal-Mart, Kroger, or the Dollar Store, and to create an activity with that item. They are also encouraged to make use of local resources such as garage sales and public libraries. Many Model Program schools have purchased textbook and workbook materials from target language countries or tapes, videos and computer software appropriate for the FLES units.

   8. **Evaluation both of student achievement and of program success.** The Georgia Department of Education has seen that both

types of evaluation have been conducted on the Model Program and its students. In 1995, the Center for Applied Linguistics (CAL) evaluated the program design and its delivery. In 1997, 1998, and 2001, CAL researchers assessed Model Program students' speaking and listening comprehension skills. They administered either their Elementary Language Learner Oral Proficiency Assessment (ELLOPA) instrument to the kindergarten students or their Student Oral Proficiency Assessment (SOPA) instrument for students in grades 1-5. The assessments showed positive results in all areas and will be discussed in detail in Chapter 4.

9. **Staffing by teachers who are certified in elementary methodology and whose language skilss are at least at the advanced level of proficiency in their foreign language as rated by ACTFL's Oral Proficiency Interview.** The only clear renewable certification in foreign languages in Georgia is for grades P-12 (pre-kindergarten through twelfth grade). The state currently requires that foreign language teachers take a course in the methodology of teaching foreign languages in the elementary school. Therefore, Model Program teachers who have a Clear Renewable Georgia teaching certificate or who are provisionally certified and are working toward full certification, must all have course work in elementary school foreign language methodology. Georgia is currently feeling the effects of the nationwide shortage of teachers and has instigated a program of bringing certified elementary school teachers from target language countries to teach in the program. These teachers, as well as new hires who have not had the P-8 methods class, take an intensive summer training class sponsored by the Georgia Department of Education. If they do not take the P-8 class itself at this time, they must take it as soon as possible. Permanent certification in Georgia also requires that teachers pass language-specific portions of the Praxis II exams, and the permit certification requires a minimum rating of Advanced on ACTFL's Oral Proficiency Interview. Excellent language skills are a necessity since Model Program teachers are required to teach 98-100% in the target language. In addition, the Model Program teachers are encouraged to participate in summer study-abroad programs or state sponsored intensive language and pedagogy classes offered in or outside of Georgia in order to increase their fluency and knowledge of the culture.

10. **Continuing professional development.** This is a strong point of the Model Program which benefits from a certain amount of funding being devoted to teacher training and development. In addition to the language and culture courses mentioned above, each summer the state specialist for foreign languages organizes intensive training sessions during which some of the top experts in elementary school foreign language pedagogy serve as teachers and facilitators. In addition, there are daylong or weekend meetings during the school year where Model Program teach-

ers can assemble to discuss issues, update the curriculum, and share ideas and materials. Cross-site observations promote the sharing of ideas between the teachers and provide modeling for new teachers.

11. School and community support. The Model Program has strong support from its school administrators and from parents. A 1995 study by the Center for Applied Linguistics found that there was strong school and community support for the Model Program. A specific example of this is that in one Model Program school, parents, teachers and students all work together each spring on a foreign language carnival. They earn money to partially support a trip to France during spring vacation for fifth grade French students and some of their teachers and parents. The school has had three such trips. Parents and teachers are also strong advocates for foreign languages for their children. Each time that Model Program funding has been threatened, parents have written and called their legislators to request continued funding for the program. Recently, parents, teachers, university professors, district and state administrators as well as members of the business community have joined together to form the Georgia Coalition on Language Learning. This group has been very influential in convincing legislators to add the Model Program funding back into the state budget when monies were cut on two occasions.

12. Cultural awareness and understanding are explicit goals of the program. The ninth statement of the Model Program *Philosophy and Pedagogy* says that teachers are committed to "seek ways to include meaningful culture content in every lesson and in every unit" (Georgia Department of Education, Curriculum Services, 2002a). The teachers make an effort to incorporate culturally authentic materials. For example, a French teacher had her first-grade students use a laminated version of a French pupil's book bag, a *cartable*, in order to study classroom objects. Japanese students have used origami animals to study different animal species and they have used chopsticks to try a Japanese dish. Spanish students have looked at pictures of markets found in various Spanish-speaking nations and they have tasted the fruits and vegetables native to these countries. German teachers have used authentic fairy tales when studying the responsibility of family members. All language classrooms incorporate authentic songs, stories and childhood chants.

CONCLUSION

Why is this discussion of theory, programs and methodology so important? It is to show that the Model Program is deeply rooted in theory and it reflects up-to-date knowledge of best practices in foreign language education. It is a well-thought-out program formulated with input from leading experts in the field of foreign language methodology. Those parents and/or educators who desire to implement a foreign language program at their elementary schools will want to select a program that is based on good theory, is appropriate for their young children and offers the best examples of good methodology. The original intent of the Model Program was that it serve as a model upon which other schools and districts could design their elementary school foreign language programs. In this it has succeeded. In referring to the Georgia Model Program, Carol Ann Pesola Dahlberg (2003) has stated that it is "the best of the FLES model." In Chapter 2 we have tried to lay out the basis on which the Georgia Elementary School Foreign Languages Model Program is a design worthy of emulation. It is a model in the truest sense of the word.

CHAPTER 3

THE CURRICULUM

INTRODUCTION

The main strength of any educational program lies in its curriculum. It is particularly important in an elementary school foreign language program that the curriculum be well designed because, in most cases, there is no textbook and the curriculum is the only guide to appropriate instruction. Without a tested, articulated, usable curriculum, classroom interaction can become a series of independent activities on topics such as colors, numbers, weather and the like, with no unified educational goal or theme. A casual visitor to an elementary school foreign language class may see students engaged in games, Total Physical Response (TPR) activities, singing and other fun activities and may come away with the idea that foreign language learning is a compendium of frivolous activities. However, under an appropriate thematic curriculum, each of these "fun" activities serves a purpose and is designed to meet an educational objective. Chapter 3 will describe the curriculum used in the Georgia Elementary School Foreign Languages Model Program. The Model Program's K-5 curriculum was incorporated into Georgia's state curriculum, the *Quality Core Curriculum* (QCC), in 1998 and can be accessed through the World Wide Web at www.glc.k12.ga.us.[1] Chapter 3 describes how the curriculum is thematically webbed, and it explains the various curriculum components: objectives, progress indicators, structures, vocabulary and assessment recommendations. The chapter concludes with an example, prepared by a third grade Spanish teacher, of how to use the curriculum for planning a unit of instruction.

CURRICULUM COMPONENTS

Thematic Web

In the early stages of the development of the Model Program, the curriculum consisted solely of objectives of what students should be able to do. Later, vocabulary lists were added in order to give guidance to teachers. Not long after the program began, upon the recommendation of Carol Ann Pesola Dahlberg, co-author of *Languages and Children: Making the Match* (1994), a thematic approach to curriculum and lesson planning was added. The Model Program curriculum became unified under a thematic web. The web design includes topics that are cognitively appropriate for elementary school children. As mentioned in Chapter 2, Piaget's (1963) research showed that most elementary school children tend to be egocentric; that is, they view the world in terms of their own, immediate environment. Reflecting this aspect of children's cognitive development, the center of the thematic web for all six years of the Model Program curriculum is *The World of the Child*. The third grade web, located in Figure 3.1, is representative of the thematic webs found in each grade level. The four overarching themes are: *All About Me*, *My School*, *My Community*, and *The Wide, Wide World*. In keeping with what we know about how children perceive their world, these themes begin with the child's most immediate environment, his or her home and family, and interconnect with other areas familiar to children: their school, their community and the wider world. A look at the thematic web for third grade gives an idea of the types of topics treated under each web theme. Using the *All About Me* web theme, teachers prepare students to talk about themselves, their families, pets, hobbies and eating habits. The *My School* web theme allows them to talk about the school year, their own course subjects and daily schedules. Students address the people and places around them by using the *My Community* web theme; and they learn map skills, study such topics as the solar system and animal habitats and compare their homes to target culture homes under *The Wide, Wide World* web theme. The thematic webs help guide the foreign language teachers by providing topics and content appropriate for each grade level. They also help teachers avoid inappropriate and interest-devoid "units" on discrete topics such as colors or numbers by offering

Early Language Learning: A Model for Success 43

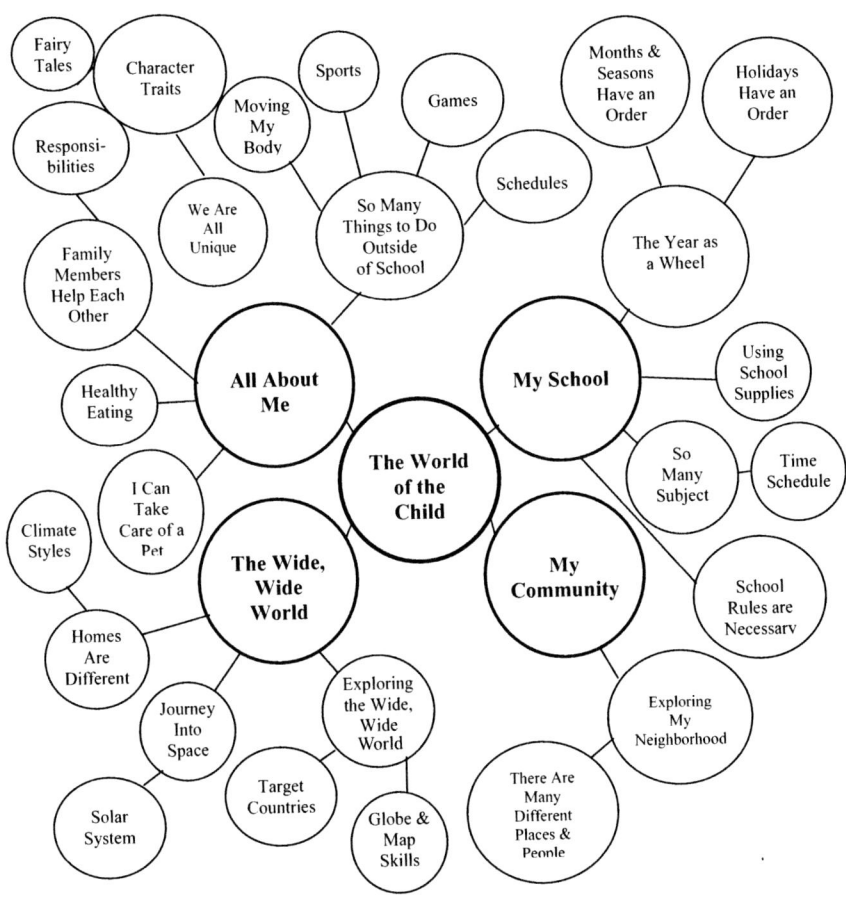

Curriculum Web ESFL Model Program: 3rd Grade

Source: Georgia Department of Education, Curriculum Services, 2000.

Figure 3.1. Thematic Web for Third Grade

suggestions for more meaning-enriched units. For example, during the third grade unit, *I Can Take Care of a Pet*, students can review or learn new colors to describe their pets and can use math skills to graph the number or types of pets owned by members of the class and to add up the cost of pet care items found in a pet store.

We will now examine the individual components found in the Model Program curriculum. A complete section of the *Foreign Language Grade K-5 Curriculum* for the third grade web theme, *All About Me*, is located in

Appendix E. Readers can refer to this appendix while reading about the various components described in the following section.

Vocabulary and Recommended Structures

The Quality Core Curriculum includes both vocabulary and functional structure recommendations for each thematic topic. Although the vocabulary is provided to the teachers in lists, the Model Program's statement of its *Philosophy and Pedagogy* explicitly states that teachers should "present vocabulary in chunks and in context rather than as isolated words or lists" (Georgia Department of Education, Curriculum Services, 2002a). The vocabulary is recycled and expanded upon each year. For instance, kindergarten students are to learn just five family member words: mother, father, sister, brother, baby. In first grade, the curriculum adds extended family members such as grandmother, grandfather, aunt and so on. In second grade, the vocabulary focuses on describing family members, and by third grade, the web devoted to the family recycles family members with the responsibilities they have at home such as to clean, to cut the grass, or to wash the dishes. The fourth and fifth grade webs are supported by thematic scenarios with topics such as *The Family in Fairy Tales* that recycle the family members using them as a basis to describe character traits in target language stories.

The curriculum for each grade-level web theme includes a list of the main structures that students can be expected to use for the theme. An examination of the theme of family shows some representative structures for first grade, such as, "My name is _____," "I have _____," "He/she is _____." The third grade structures on the same topic are more advanced including: "We have _____," "My _____ likes to _____." Once again, these structures are to be integrated into the context as the need for them arises in meaningful communication and not to be studied as parsed out grammar.

One of the benefits of the web topics and the lists of vocabulary and structures is to help the foreign language teachers *limit the focus* of what they present in the first few years. Because national and state experts as well as experienced elementary school foreign language teachers construct, implement and revise the curriculum, it provides a realistic guide as to what and how much is appropriate at each level. First grade teachers will have clear recommendations for the vocabulary and structures seven-year-olds can handle and will not overwhelm the students with too much information and vocabulary. Teachers of the upper elementary grades will know what vocabulary and structures to recycle with a brief review versus what is new and needs more thorough presentation and practice.

Progress Indicators

The section named *Progress Indicators* includes a list of specific thematic and/or content-related goals directly associated with each web theme. The Progress Indicators for a web theme are all listed together, and it is up to the teacher to choose the ones appropriate for the unit he or she is planning. For instance, when we look again at the third grade curriculum guide for *All About Me*, if a teacher is planning to teach a unit on *So Many Things to Do Outside of School*, he or she could incorporate the following three progress indicators into the unit:

Progress Indicator 3: Students will provide autobiographical information in oral and written forms;

Progress Indicator 4: Students will report on activities outside of school; and

Progress Indicator 5: Students will determine which body parts are exercised in certain games and/or sports activities.

If a teacher is doing the unit on *Healthy Eating*, he or she would use:

Progress Indicator 6: Students will identify selected foods in the native and target cultures and categorize them according to mealtimes; and

Progress Indicator 7: Students will describe and discuss a balanced meal using the food pyramid (Georgia Department of Education, Curriculum Services, 2002b).

Progress indicators are similar to language objectives but differ in that they relate directly to each theme of the curriculum while the objectives, described in the next section, relate to global language use.

Language Objectives

The objectives for the Georgia Elementary School Foreign Languages Model Program are found online, and the complete list of the third grade objectives is located in Appendix E. The objectives are stated in terms of language expectations and are repeated with slight modifications and additions as students progress from grade to grade. Note, for instance, the articulation of similar speaking objectives from kindergarten through fifth grade.

Students will be able to:

K.22: Use words and high frequency utterances to attempt communication. (1.1)

1.21: Use a limited number of words and phrases on a variety of familiar topics. (1.1)

2.23: Use a limited number of words and phrases on a variety of topics. (1.1)

3.24: Maintain simple conversations in the present tense on a variety of simple topics. (1.1)

4.24: Maintain simple conversations in the present tense at the sentence level on a variety of familiar topics, with some efforts at expressing past and future tense. (1.1)

5.25: Maintain simple conversations in the present tense at the sentence level on a variety of familiar topics, with some efforts at expressing past and future tense. (1.1) (Georgia Department of Education, Curriculum Services 2002b).

The objectives address comprehension, speaking, reading, writing, cultural understanding and comparisons, content-related knowledge and lifelong learning. Some objectives, omitted in early grades, are added in later grade levels, others are expanded upon and modified as the students progress in both language skills and cognitive maturity. For instance, there is no objective related to knowledge of language structures in kindergarten. In first grade, students "begin to recognize limited language structures," and in second through fifth grades, students "use linguistic patterns in limited monitoring of speech and writing" (Georgia Department of Education, Curriculum Services, 2002b).

National Standards

In 1996, the *Standards for Foreign Language Learning in the 21st Century* (National Standards in Foreign Language Education Project, 1996) were first published. There are 11 standards centered around five areas, known as the five Cs: Communication, Cultures, Connections, Comparisons Communities. The numbers in parentheses at the end of each language objective in the curriculum give the number of the standard best reflected by that objective. The objectives reflect all 11 of the national standards. Table 3.1 shows a sampling from third grade of how the objectives reflect the national standards. It is clear that one of the strengths of the Model Program curriculum is that it is standards-based. The national standards for foreign language learning are addressed by the language objectives and content-related standards are addressed by the progress indicators.

Table 3.1. How National Standards for Foreign Language Learning are Addressed in the Quality Core Curriculum

National Standard Number	Short Description of Standard	Objective Number	QCC Objective
1.1	Interpersonal Communication	3.12	Ask for information and make requests of teachers and other language speakers.
1.2	Interpretive Communication	3.3	Read to find needed information.
1.3	Presentational Communication	3.10	Use the target language for a variety of extended spoken activities, such as skits, dialogues, plays, poems, research reports for a variety of audiences.
2.1	Cultural Practices and Perspectives	3.22	Use culturally appropriate language and behavior in both formal and informal target language situations (greeting, leave-taking, eating customs, travel, school, etc.)
2.2	Cultural Products and Perspectives	3.25	Participate actively in classroom experiences with music, sports, games, songs, dance or musical instruments from the target culture, and extend these experiences into their personal lives.
3.1	Connections to Other Disciplines	3.23	Use the target language in appropriate content-related areas including, but not limited to, mathematics, social studies, science, literature and fine arts.
3.2	Gain Information Using the Target Language	3.26	Use information gained through the target language and cultures to satisfy personal needs and interests.
4.1	Language Comparisons	3.31	Recognize linguistic patterns that occur in the foreign language and compare them with native language patterns.
4.2	Cultural Comparisons	3.20	Identify, compare and contrast diverse cultural practices and products, including language, emphasizing similarities as well as differences.
5.1	Use Target Language Beyond School	3.25	Participate actively in classroom experiences with music, sports, games, songs, dance or musical instruments from the target culture, and extend these experiences into their personal lives.
5.2	Lifelong Learning	3.27	Begin to identify work-related applications of language proficiency.

Assessment Recommendations

The Model Program's curriculum offers assessment recommendations that coordinate with each of the language objectives. These recommendations are not intended to be comprehensive or prescriptive but are suggested examples of appropriate activities teachers could use to assess pupil performance on each objective. For example, looking at third grade again, for objective 3.4, "Write using sentences or clusters of language," the corresponding assessment is also labeled 3.4 "Create big books by writing brief summaries of familiar stories, fairy tales, or topics of personal interest and illustrating them." Teachers are not constrained to create big books or to read fairy tales but can design a similar assessment activity that reflects the theme and objectives of the particular unit under study.

USING THE CURRICULUM TO PLAN A UNIT OF INSTRUCTION

It is one thing to look at the QCC online and take note of its components when planning a unit of instruction. It is another to pull the various components together into a coherent whole and to construct a workable unit to be implemented in a particular classroom. The best way to demonstrate this process is to examine an actual unit plan based on the Model Program curriculum. How a teacher approaches implementing the curriculum for a specific unit will depend on the age of the pupils, the background of the teacher and the availability of materials to scaffold the instruction. In earlier grades, teachers frequently use songs or stories as organizers for a unit. Adaptations of old familiar favorites such as *Goldilocks and the Three Bears* or *The Very Hungry Caterpillar* (Carle, 1987) can capture the pupils' interest when teaching units incorporating the family, rooms of the house or foods. Or authentic books from the target culture can add both story form and cultural enrichment. Songs, too, both familiar and from the target culture, can offer unit planning ideas for the younger grades. Since young children live in a world surrounded by fantasy, it is imperative for the teacher to plan instruction to capture the students' imaginations. Younger children, pre-K through second grade, acquire their language while engaged in activities that spark their imaginations.

In later grades students prefer more mature approaches, and the teacher can become less reliant on stories or songs that the older children may consider too babyish. Older students also need and want more to say. While it is appropriate for younger learners to name and identify or to respond to the teacher in short phrases, we are doing our older learners a disservice if we do not provide the means for them to use more extended language. This does not mean demanding that everything students say has to be in complete sentences, but it does mean providing them a means to initiate and sustain conversation themselves. The older students are at an age where they can become less teacher-dependent and can begin working with a partner or in small groups on tasks that enable them to interact with each other. The third through fifth grade teachers must plan for and implement ways to get the older children to use extended language. Sometimes it is a difficult transition for a teacher who is used to being in charge, directing the activities, to give up this control and to allow students to work with each other. It takes careful planning and appropriate scaffolding, such as guided conversations, flip up posters, question and phrase banks (not just word banks) and guided compositions.

The following is an example of a third grade Spanish unit, written by Joe Frank Uriz, that demonstrates a way to plan for the extended language use described above. Joe teaches at a school in a large metropolitan area in Georgia that has a diverse, multiethnic enrollment of around 400 students who begin their Spanish instruction in kindergarten. Joe wrote the unit when he was completing his certification program at Georgia State University, and he followed the unit plan guidelines required by his university supervisor, Carol M. Saunders Semonsky. Joe's complete unit plan is located in Appendix F. We will examine Joe's planning sequence step by step.

Coordination of Information from the Quality Core Curriculum

The preliminary steps 1-6 make direct use of the Model Program curriculum found on the Georgia Quality Core Curriculum website.

Step 1:   Look at the third grade thematic web and decide on a topic. Joe chose the topic, *I Can Take Care of a Pet*, from the web theme *All About Me*.

Step 2:   Look at the curriculum for *All About Me* to locate progress indicators supporting the topic. Joe found the following progress indicators relating to his unit on pet care:

Progress indicator 3.1:   Students will describe, compare and contrast responsibilities of different family members at home.

Progress indicator 3.2:   Students will identify and summarize various components of pet care.

Progress indicator 3.3: Students will provide autobiographical information in oral and written form.

Progress indicator 3.4: Students will report on activities outside of school.

Step 3: Examine related progress indicators in grades K-2 to determine what needs to be recycled. Joe found these related progress indicators from previous grades:

Progress indicator K.2: Students will recognize and identify a selected number of household pets.

Progress indicator 1.6: Students will identify and name different pets.

Progress indicator 1.7: Students will describe similarities and differences of various pets.

Step 4: Look at the vocabulary suggested for third grade as well as at related vocabulary presented in K-2 to determine what to review and what will be new for the students. Related third grade vocabulary is:

to describe	to compare	to contrast	to work
to take care of	responsibilities	to have to	to feed
to wash/to bathe	veterinarian	shot	bone
leash	collar	basket	toys
cage	dish	tank	to buy
full	empty	to exercise	to need
to want			

Vocabulary to be recycled from K-2:

dog	cat	bird	rabbit
fish	turtle	animal	pet
snake			

Do you have a pet? Its name is ___
My ___ is the color ___ What is your favorite pet?
My favorite pet is ___ My ___'s name is ___

Step 5: Look at the recommended structures for third grade as well as those to review from grades K-2. Recommended structures from grade 3 are:

It is ___ and/or ___ It is ___, not ___
I am (verb) He/she/it is (verb)

We are (verb)
I like to/don't like to (verb) + (objective)
(subject) + (verb) + always/never/sometimes
Who does (verb)?
Who (verb)?
My ___ is ___
I have ___ and ___
They have ___ and ___
My ___ needs ___
I am going to ___

They are (verb)

I do (verb)
I (verb)
My ___ is ___, not ___
He/she/it has ___ and ___
My ___ likes to ___
I like to ___
I want ___

Structures recycled from K-2:

I would like ___
___ is too ___
___ is ___er (comparative)
It/that/this is
My/mine
the/a/an
He/she/it is ___ years old

Do you want?
There is/there are ___
___ is ___est (superlative)
I/me
you/your
___ is not ___
for/in/from/on/with

Step 6: Select the language objectives for grade 3 to be reinforced in this unit. This will be cross checked after the activities for the unit have been planned.

Additional Idea Gathering

Now that all the components from the curriculum have been examined and analyzed, it is time to begin more specific planning. It is here where individual teachers will use the information gathered from the curriculum along with their own unique language and cultural background experiences to construct their own, individualized unit plans. There are several steps the teacher takes in order to generate a richer unit with meaningful activities. These are the steps recommended to pre-service and in-service teachers by Carol M. Saunders Semonsky from Georgia State University who serves as a consultant in curriculum planning for the Model Program teachers.

Step 7: Form a content-related web to make connections between the unit topic and other content subject areas. See Curtain and Pesola (1994) for more on content-related planning. This enriches the unit by letting the teacher brainstorm how to incorporate activities that stretch across the curriculum. Joe's content-related web can be found in Figure 3.2. A look at Joe's web indicates many connections, including those to math (the

52 The Curriculum

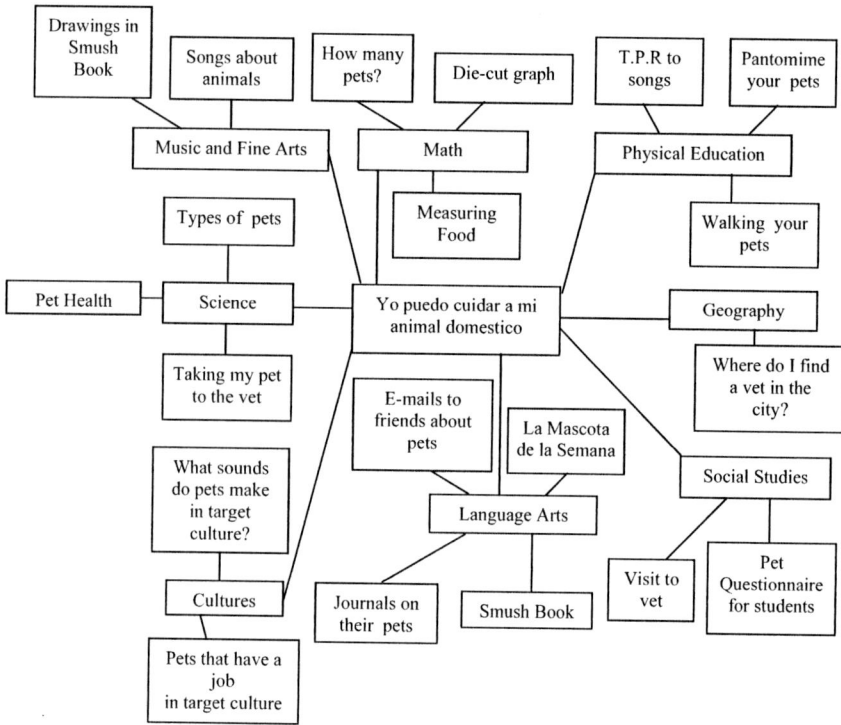

Source: Joe Frank Uriz.

Figure 3.2. Joe's Content-related Web

shopping at a pet store activity where students add up the cost of what is bought), science (size, colors and needs of different pet species), music (many songs related to animals), social studies and culture (several of the songs are from the target culture, and Joe touches on how pets are treated in the families of target culture children), language arts (guided writing, reading the Pet of the Week website), physical education (various TPR activities), and art (students draw their own or an imaginary pet).

Step 8: Look for songs related to the topic to incorporate into the unit. Joe, having been raised in a Spanish-speaking environment and having visited target language countries, had a selection of authentic songs that he knew. If this is not the situation, there are other avenues of finding authentic songs: consultation with native speakers, research on the Internet, and review of various commercial cassette tapes and compact discs are a few suggestions. The teacher is urged to make up songs to melodies that are familiar to the students (*Mary Had a Little Lamb* and the like). If the commercial cassettes have both the target language and English the teacher can edit them by retaping desired portions without the English.

Step 9: Think of Total Physical Response (TPR) (Asher, 1986) activities, Gouin series and other movement games to incorporate. Joe incorporated TPR on animal movements.

Step 10: Look for authentic stories that relate to the theme. If the language is too complicated for the students' level, the teacher can modify the language. Teachers can also construct their own big books or felt story boards to use in developing their own story line. This step may take place earlier in the unit planning sequence if a teacher has a particular story that lends itself well to the unit topic. In this case, he may want to use this book as the story-form organizer (Curtain & Pesola, 1994). For instance, a Model Program French teacher used a children's book, *Bon Appétit, Monsieur Lapin!* (Boujon, 1985) as the unit organizer for his second-grade unit that included describing the color and texture of fruits and vegetables.

Step 11: Make a list of games and materials on hand and begin to generate a bigger list of what will be needed. The teacher will add to the list of materials after planning the unit activities. Joe chose a wide selection of games and materials, including Internet sites, that we will describe below.

PUTTING IT ALL TOGETHER: BACKWARDS PLANNING

Following the ideas of Grant Wiggins and Jay McTighe (1998), we recommend using the concept of backwards planning when preparing a unit. Under this paradigm, teachers begin the planning process by determining the overarching objectives they want the students to achieve and by deciding at the onset what methods of assessment will be used to determine if the objectives have been accomplished. In his foreign language methods classes, Joe had been required to state these overarching objectives in terms of "Extended Language Use Objectives." This requirement leads teachers to focus on meaningful language use by the students rather than on discrete identification and naming as the end goal. Joe therefore began his planning process with his "Extended Language Use Objectives" and the "Overarching Assessment Activities" he would use to determine student performance of the objectives. Table 3.2 shows Joe's two overarching objectives and their accompanying assessments for his unit. Joe decided on two extended language objectives, one in which the students describe their pets and how to take care of them, and the other, in which students describe going to the vet. For his two objectives, Joe planned three possible assessment activities. For the first objective, he had both a written assessment, a guided writing assignment where students describe the "Pet of the Week" taken from a website in Spanish, and an oral assessment where the students present their real or imaginary pet to the class. For his second extended language objective, Joe's students would be asked to perform a skit about "Going to the Veterinarian." By delineating up front what he expected from his students by the end of the unit, Joe could now construct a series of activities all designed to lead the students to successfully accomplish the planned assessments. All of his introductory and expansion activities funnel down to the overarching assessments. In elementary school foreign language classes, where there is often no textbook, it is up to the teacher to devise an appropriate unit of instruction on his or her own. This can be a challenge, especially to new teachers or to those not used to working creatively from a curriculum guide. Frequently, the inexperienced teachers offer a "tossed salad" approach to their lessons. They plan a variety of discrete, teacher-directed, non-related activities which may include some basic categories such as colors, numbers, weather, family and the like. Students will parrot or learn to provide appropriate responses, but there is little connected, meaningful language in use. Through training in how to use the thematic curriculum effectively, and in how to organize activities all to focus on a preplanned overarching goal, even the newest teacher is able to plan meaningful units of instruction. This is why knowledge of the curriculum components and of the notion of backwards planning is so important.

After teachers have decided on their broad language objectives and assessments, they can begin to plan activities that will enable pupils to be successful at the assessments. Since Joe had already done the preliminary work of deciding what vocabulary, progress indicators and structures he wanted to address, as well as preparing his content-related web, he could now proceed to plan his individual activities. Because Joe prepared this unit as part of a work sample required for his internship experience at

Table 3.2. Joe Frank's Broad Language Objectives and Overarching Assessment Activities

Broad Language Objectives	*Overarching Language Assessments*
1. Students will describe their pets and the responsibilities in caring for their pet.	1a) *La Mascota de la Semana* (formal written assessment)
	1b) Skit Presentations: Students Present Their Pets (formal oral assessment: option 1)
2. Students will describe "going to the vet"	2. Skit Presentations: Going to the Vet (formal oral assessment: option 2)

Georgia State University, he followed the unit plan designed by Carol M. Saunders Semonsky for student teachers. The unit plans students in the teacher education program must write are much more detailed than what would be expected of a teacher in the classroom. This is because students must demonstrate to the professor what their thought processes are while full time teachers will have these thought processes in place. In this unit plan, the student teachers divide their activities into two sections, "Introductory Identification Activities" and "Extended Language Use Activities." The student teachers and interns must also state what scaffolding they will use in order to present the activity without the use of English in a manner that their pupils will understand.

Scaffolding is a term that refers to anything teachers do to organize and support knowledge and make it accessible to their students, and it is critical that a foreign language teacher understand this concept and how to implement it the classroom. In foreign language classes there are many forms of scaffolding. Language scaffolding is one of the most prevalent. This has been described as "teacherese" or "foreigner talk" (Curtain & Pesola, 1994, pp. 56-57). Basically, it is any modifications to the language the teacher uses to make it more understandable to students: a slightly slower speech rate, more repetition and rephrasing, use of more cognates and simple structures and frequent comprehension checks. Scaffolding can also be visual (pictures, flash cards, realia, videos), tactile (objects), aural (sound effects, voice modulation and intensity, audio tapes), kinesthetic (gestures, facial expressions) and even olfactory and gustatory (students smell cinnamon and Roquefort cheese or taste sweet, salty or sour foods). Without an ability to scaffold the target language teachers may resort to English to get their point across. So, along with the description of the activity itself, the teacher must plan how to scaffold the language to help make it comprehensible to the students.

In the first stage of planning, the teachers plan how to review and recycle previously learned material and how to present and provide initial practice on the new concepts. It is in this section that teachers plan activities centering around vocabulary identification, repetition and practice of new structures. In the second phase, the extended language use stage, teachers plan for extended, meaningful use of the language. This parsing out of stages might not be needed by an experienced teacher who is familiar with the goal of meaningful language in context. However, too many times inexperienced teachers focus on easy-to-prepare, teacher-focused activities that require pupils only to name, identify, or respond to the teacher. The pupils are never encouraged to go beyond identifying to experiment with extended communication. The authors have transferred the activities from Joe's unit plan into Table 3.3 so readers can see how Joe's activities progress from introductory to extended language use and

Table 3.3. Unit Outline for *I Can Take Care of a Pet*

Introductory Identification Activities

Introductory Identification Activity	Description and Scaffolding (in bold)	QCC Objectives	Content- or Culture-related Areas	Multiple Intelligences	National Standards
Introduction of Sr. Uriz's pet photos	Sr. Uriz shares his **pet photos** with the class, describing them and telling their names with **sentence strips**. Students respond to teacher's questions.	3.7 Demonstrate comprehension of extended oral discourse	Reading: sentence strips Science: animal descriptions	Spatial Verbal Interpersonal	1.1 Interpersonal communication 1.2 Interpretive communication 3.1 Connect to other content areas
Mystery basket of pets	Students go to the mystery basket to pull out **plush pets**. On chart paper the teacher has **sentence models** of type of animal, color, and sounds. Students mimic the animals and describe them.	3.7 Demonstrate comprehension of extended oral discourse 3.13 Provide information and make requests of teachers and other language speakers.	Reading: sentence strips Science: animal descriptions Culture: animal sounds in Spanish	Kinesthetic Verbal	3.1 Connect to other content areas 4.2 Cultural comparisons
Felt pet identification story	Teacher uses a **felt board** and **felt pets** to tell a story to introduce new pets. Students manipulate felt pets to demonstrate comprehension and to help identify them.	3.7 Demonstrate comprehension of extended oral discourse	Language Arts: listen to story	Kinesthetic Verbal	1.2 Interpretive communication
Animal Concentration Game	Students use 8 x 11" **flash cards** of pictures of pets in duplicate. Students turn over 2 cards, saying the name of the animal on each card, attempting to make a match. Points are given for a match.	3.13 Provide information and respond to requests 3.25 Participate actively in classroom experiences such as games		Spatial Verbal Interpersonal	1.1 Interpersonal communication

Activity	Description		Content	Intelligences	Standards
Mystery Trunk (*Yo puedo cuidar...*)	Teacher presents students with a decorated mystery trunk of **stuffed animals, pet care items** and **pictures** related to the responsibilities in caring for a pet. Without looking, students choose an item from the trunk and name it. It is passed around so other students can also name the item.	3.7 Demonstrate comprehension of extended oral discourse 3.13 Provide information and respond to requests	Science: pet care	Kinesthetic Verbal Interpersonal	1.1 Interpersonal communication 3.1 Connect to other content areas
Mystery Trunk Extension Activity	Using the **items selected from the trunk** and referring to **written models on sentence strips**, students formulate sentences such as, "My dog needs a leash," or "My fish needs food."	3.13 Provide information and make requests of teachers 3.14 Communicate orally using sentences	Science: pet care Reading: sentence strips	Kinesthetic Verbal Naturalist Interpersonal	1.1 Interpersonal communication 3.1 Connect to other content areas
Taking Care of a Pet TPR	The teacher, prompting with **gestures** as necessary, gives commands for taking care of a pet ("Feed the cat, walk the dog"). Students act out the commands. More advanced students then give the commands to their peers.	3.7 Demonstrate comprehension of extended discourse 3.15 Follow and give complex instructions	Science: pet care	Interpersonal Kinesthetic Verbal	1.1 Interpersonal 1.3 Interpretive communication 3.1 Connect to other content areas
Die Cut Pet Graph	Students are asked by the teacher to name their own or an imaginary pet. Students are given **die cut animals** of their pets to place on a **shower curtain graph** according to pet category. Students count, compare and contrast the number of various pets.	3.6 Summarize personal information 3.7 Demonstrate comprehension of extended oral discourse 3.13 Provide information and respond to requests 3.23 Use the target language in content-related activities	Math: graphing and counting	Kinesthetic Logical/math Spatial Verbal Interpersonal	1.1 Interpersonal communication 1.2 Interpretive communication 3.1 Connect to other content areas

(continued)

Table 3.3. Continued

Introductory Identification Activities

Introductory Identification Activity	Description and Scaffolding (in bold)	QCC Objectives	Content- or Culture-related Areas	Multiple Intelligences	National Standards
Overhead Animal Pie Game (from Scott Frederickson)	The teacher prepares **transparencies of various animal care scenes** such as a boy washing his dog or a girl feeding her fish. This is covered by a "pie," a piece of solid paper or a paper plate cut into eight triangular pie slices. Students come up and lift a piece of the pie to reveal a portion underneath. The first team to guess the picture, wins.	3.13 Provide information and respond to requests 3.25 Participate actively in classroom experiences such as games	Art: picture identification	Kinesthetic Spatial Verbal Interpersonal	1.1 Interpersonal communication 3.1 Connect to other content areas

Extended Language Use Activities

Extended Language Use Activity	Description and Scaffolding (in bold)	QCC Objectives	Content- or Culture-related Areas	Multiple Intelligences	National Standards
Classroom Pet/ Animal Center Activity	Students will have a classroom pet (fish) and keep a weekly log about the pet. The first week, students draw a picture of the animal. Using a **guided writing handout** and the posted **sentence strips**, students keep a weekly log telling how they have cared for the pet and noting any changes.	3.4 Write using clusters of language 3.6 Summarize research based on models 3.14 Communicate in writing using sentences 3.23 Use the target language in content-related activities	Art: drawing Language Arts: writing Science: pet care	Spatial Verbal Naturalist	3.1 Connect to other content areas
Guided Questionnaires and Interviews about Pets	Students, using a **prepared questionnaire**, respond to questions about their own or imaginary pets. Then, they interview peers about their pets and jot down their partners' responses. Students summarize their partners' responses and present to the class.	3.10 Use the target language for a variety of extended spoken activities 3.12 Ask for information and make requests of teachers and other language speakers 3.13 Provide information and respond to requests 3.24 Maintain simple conversations in the present tense on familiar topics 3.28 Attempt to create with the language at the sentence level 3.29 Draw from a basic vocabulary that permits exchanges of a personal nature 3.32 Use linguistic patterns in limited monitoring of speech and writing	Science: pet care Language Arts: writing and reading	Interpersonal Intrapersonal Verbal	1.1 Interpersonal communication 1.3 Presentational communication 3.1 Connect to other content areas 4.1 Language comparisons

(continued)

Table 3.3. Continued

Extended Language Use Activities

Extended Language Use Activity	Description and Scaffolding (in bold)	QCC Objectives	Content- or Culture-related Areas	Multiple Intelligences	National Standards
Pet Journals	Students, working in pairs using their **guided questionnaire responses**, complete a chart of their own and their partners' pets. Then, using a **guided writing page**, they journal about their own and their friends' pets.	3.4 Write using sentences or clusters of language 3.5 Write short texts on topics of personal interest 3.6 Summarize personal information based on models 3.14 Communicate orally and in writing using sentences 3.28 Attempt to create with the language at the sentence level 3.29 Draw from a basic vocabulary that permits exchanges of a personal nature 3.32 Use linguistic patterns in limited monitoring of speech and writing	Language Arts: journal writing	Interpersonal Intrapersonal Verbal	1.1 Interpersonal communication 1.3 Presentational communication 3.1 Connect to other content areas 4.1 Language comparisons
Kidpix software computer lab	Students use **Kidpix software** to design a slide show of taking care of their pet, writing sentences for each slide. Students use their **pet journals** as a scaffold. Students present their slide shows to their peers.	Objectives as listed in the previous activity (3.4, 3.5, 3.6, 3.14, 3.28, 3.29, 3.32); Also: 3.10 Use the target language for a variety of extended spoken activities	Language Arts: writing Science: Pet care Technology: slide show software	Intrapersonal Verbal	1.3 Presentational Communication 3.1 Connect to other content areas

Writing E-mails to Friends or Family	Students, using a **printout of their slide show**, write a guided letter to a keypal about their pets.	Objectives as listed in the previous activity (3.4, 3.5, 3.6, 3.14, 3.28, 3.29, 3.32)	Language Arts: letter writing Technology: E-mail	Interpersonal Intrapersonal Verbal	1.1 Interpersonal Communication 5.1 Language use within and beyond school
Smush Book: *Mi Mascota*	Students construct a Smush Book by cutting and folding a piece of white paper. Using the **teacher's book as a model**, for each of the eight pages of the book, students draw a picture of their pet and its needs, writing a corresponding sentence underneath. They read their books to peers and parents.	Objectives as listed previously (3.4, 3.5, 3.6, 3.10, 3.14, 3.28, 3.29, 3.32); Also: 3.2 Read linguistically and developmentally appropriate passages 3.7 Demonstrate comprehension of extended spoken discourse 3.11 Share information of their choice with audiences outside the classroom	Art: drawing Language Arts: writing	Interpersonal Intrapersonal Spatial Verbal	1.1 Interpersonal Communication 1.2 Interpretive Communication 1.3 Presentational Communication 3.1 Connect to other content areas 4.1 Language comparisons 5.1 Language use within and beyond school
La Mascota de la Semana Internet activity This activity is also used for the formal written assessment.	Each week, students visit the **website**: http://www.yupimsn.com/yupinos/mascotas and read about the pet of the week to get information on the pet. They complete a weekly **guided journal** describing each week's pet.	Objectives as previously listed (3.4, 3.5, 3.6, 3.7, 3.14, 3.28, 3.32) Also: 3.3 Read to find needed information	Language Arts reading and journal writing Technology: Internet websites	Verbal	1.2 Interpretive communication 3.1 Connect to other content areas

(continued)

Table 3.3. Continued

Extended Language Use Activities

Extended Language Use Activity	Description and Scaffolding (in bold)	QCC Objectives	Content- or Culture-related Areas	Multiple Intelligences	National Standards
Skit presentations: "Meet my Pet" This activity is used for the formal oral assessment.	Students present a skit about taking care of their pet. Students are provided with a **hand-out describing the skit requirements.** They practice with their partners and present their skit to the class. The teacher videotapes and grades using a grading rubric.	3.4 Write using clusters of language 3.5 Write short texts on topics of personal interest 3.6 Summarize personal information 3.8 Begin to self-edit 3.10 Use the target language for a variety of extended spoken activities such as skits 3.12 Ask for information 3.13 Provide information and respond to requests 3.14 Communicate orally and in writing using sentences 3.16 Demonstrate an understanding of a variety of speech sources 3.24 Maintain simple conversations in the present tense 3.28 Attempt to create with the language at the sentence level 3.29 Draw from a basic vocabulary that permits exchanges of a personal nature 3.31 Recognize linguistic patterns that occur in the foreign language and compare them with native language patterns 3.32 Use linguistic patterns in limited monitoring of speech	Language Arts: speech and drama Science: pet care	Verbal Interpersonal Natualrist	1.1 Interpersonal Communication 1.2 Interpretive Communication 1.3 Presentational Communication 3.1 Connect to other content areas 4.1 Language Comparisons 5.1 Language use within and beyond school

how they are scaffolded. The scaffolding is highlighted in bold within the table. Joe's unit plan forms the basis for the table, but a detailed description of how his activities reflect the Georgia Quality Core Curriculum, the National Standards for Foreign Language Leaning as well as multiple intelligences and culture and content-related areas have been added. We wish to point out that this table is much more complex and detailed than the unit plan a teacher would realistically write. It is designed to show how teacher-planned activities reflect the curriculum and standards.

Joe planned his unit for a three-week time frame. We see that he begins his lesson by accessing the students' background knowledge. He shows them photos of his pets and begins to describe them. At this point, the vocabulary he uses is mostly review from first and second grade. He points out the color and size of the pets in the photos as he describes them and gradually begins to expand his vocabulary a bit. He scaffolds this now by putting up sentence strips reflecting the important language he wants his students to recognize and use. He continues this introductory stage over several days, using the rest of his introductory and concept setting activities. Joe reinforces the naming review of the animals by using the "Mystery Basket of Pets" activity. First he demonstrates, using the drama of the hidden pets, by choosing a stuffed animal out of the decorated basket and naming it. Then, individual children come to the basket to choose and name the pets. The stuffed animals are handed around the class as each child has an opportunity to name the pet before it is passed on to the next child. To incorporate story form, Joe uses a felt board and constructs a story where the new pets are introduced to the existing group of pet friends. Students identify, describe and manipulate the new pets through this activity and the next one where Joe uses pictures of both the new and old pets. Building on the pictures, Joe now adds pictures and objects of items needed to take care of the pets the students have just practiced. The students use the pictures in several identification games and activities. One of the games is "Animal Concentration" where Joe has duplicate flash cards for each pet and pet item. These are large and are placed either face down on the floor, attached to the board with magnets, or in the pockets of a large shower curtain pocket chart hanging on the wall. One child at a time comes up to turn over two cards, naming the item found on the back. If the items are a match, the student gets to keep the cards and take another turn. If the items do not match, they are returned to their original places face down and another child comes up for a turn. The next activity in the sequence is the "Mystery Trunk" which is similar to the "Mystery Basket" activity. Students reach in and choose a pet care item such as a leash, fish food or a bowl. Joe provides sentence scaffolding by placing sentence strips on the board cuing the correct phrase in Spanish, "My ____ needs a ____." Joe can prompt questions,

"What does your pet need?" or "Which pet needs a leash?" More advanced students then can take over the questioning of their peers. Joe intersperses these activities with Total Physical Response kinesthetic activities related to pets, while at the same time reinforcing typical commands related to pets such as "Walk the dog, feed the fish, give water to the rabbit."

Joe includes content-related activities taken from the ideas in his content web. Seeking to incorporate mathematics, Joe plans a graphing activity. He has prepared ahead of time a large shower curtain graph with the grid made out of colored masking tape. For this graph, students name a real or imaginary pet they have at home or would like to have and are given a die cut of the pet they name. Students then come up one at a time and place their die cut pet in the correct animal category. Joe now asks the class several math-related questions. How many of each category are there? Are there more cats than dogs? How many more dogs than fish are there? Which category has the fewest pets? How many dogs and cats are there versus birds and fish? He plans a second math-related activity in the form of a worksheet. On the worksheet is a drawing of a pet store front displaying various pet care items for sale with prices in dollars and cents. Students fill in the worksheet by stating what pet they have; then, they must "buy" three items from the pet store, naming them and giving their price. Finally, they add up the cost of their items and subtract that total from the $10 they started with to determine their change. To incorporate art, Joe has the children play the "Overhead Animal Pie" game. Joe first makes several overhead transparencies of individual pets and items associated with them. These he places one at a time on the overhead before it is turned on. Over this, he constructs a pie with eight individual pie pieces out of construction paper or a cut up paper plate. He puts the pie pieces over the transparency picture to hide it, and turns on the overhead. Now, one student at a time from each team comes up and uncovers one piece of the pie. He or she can guess the animal or can confer with his or her teammates. If the guess is right that team wins; if the guess is not made or is wrong, a member of the other team comes up to remove the next piece of his or her choice. This process continues until one team identifies the picture correctly. Joe also incorporates music throughout the unit by teaching the students animal related songs as introductory or transition activities.

When he feels his students have acquired the basic vocabulary, Joe expands his focus to include activities aimed at garnering extended, chunked language. He now is activating the extended language use phase of his unit plan. Two of the activities are ongoing and recursive: the classroom pet journal and the "*Mascota de la Semana.*" For the first, Joe bought a goldfish, and the students were to keep a log on how they cared for it during the week and were to note any changes in the fish. The fish proved problematic because it died. Unbeknownst to his students, Joe replaced the fish several times. Next time he says he will try a gerbil. Art was interwoven into this activity by having the students draw the classroom pet at the beginning of their log. The second recursive activity was the "Pet of the Week" web site in Spanish. On this site there are a picture and description of a new pet every week. Joe took his students to the computer lab each week and had them fill out a guided writing form with the new information. Students loved this activity and he later used it as one of his writing assessments.

Joe planned several other activities aimed at getting the students to produce extended language; some were more successful than others. The ones that didn't succeed as planned were his e-mail activity and the Kidpix slide show. He had planned for his students to e-mail friends or family about their pets, but not every student had access to an e-mail account. Joe had to abandon this idea. The Kidpix slide show proved to be too time consuming in addition to the Pet of the Week that also had to be done in the computer lab. Joe's class met in a trailer and going into the main building to the computer lab during the 30-minute classes was not feasible for more than one computer project at a time. Several other ideas did work out well. Joe prepared a guided interview form with three columns. At the top he put cue words in Spanish: pet, name, color, size, needs. The students filled out their own information first, then interviewed two peers about their pets and recorded the information. Joe had the model questions displayed on butcher paper for those students who needed extra verbal support. Students then reported about their friends' pets to the class. Then, using their interview forms as a guide, the students expanded this activity by writing one paragraph about their own pet and one paragraph about their friends' pets. The final extended writing activity Joe's students did was to make a smush book. A smush book is a book made out of one sheet of paper that is cut to make it fold into an eight-page "book." Students drew their pet and its name on the title page. Each subsequent page contained a picture and a sentence about their pet, its needs a visit to the veterinarian.

Now that Joe had provided extensive practice in both written and oral forms, he determined that his students were prepared to perform the formal assessments. His assessment assignments and grading rubrics are found in Appendix G. All of the unit activities led up to and provided practice on skills needed for the students to be successful on the assessments. The written formal assessment, "Pet of the Week," was the same assignment that the students had already practiced several times. For the assessment, however, the pet was new and the scaffolding was reduced. That way, Joe could see what the students were able to do on their own.

For the formal oral assessment, Joe had originally planned to offer a selection of two skits. The first skit was of two friends discussing their pets and their needs, and the second was of taking a pet to the veterinarian. This second skit was not actually offered to the students at the end of the unit because Joe felt he had not provided enough practice on going to the veterinarian. So, all of Joe's students participated in the skit where they described their pets. For each formal assessment, written and oral, Joe provided students with both an assignment sheet and a grading rubric. That way students knew exactly what was expected of them and Joe was much more likely to get the kind of language he was aiming for. Joe's assessment assignments are found in Appendix G.

As part of his work sample for his internship at Georgia State University, Joe had to determine if he did, indeed, bring his students to high levels of learning. In other words, he had to assess himself and how well his students performed on the unit assessments. He determined that 88% of students met or exceeded expectations on the formal assessments. To cross-check effectiveness, Joe asked his students to fill out a questionnaire self-evaluating how well they perceived they could perform the unit objectives, taking care of a pet and describing responsibilities related to pet care. Most students verified that they had learned about pet care and could describe pets and pet needs in Spanish. In addition, Joe was observed by his university supervisor and a mentor teacher from his own school, both of whom found his lesson plans and delivery to be appropriate and effective for both cognitive level and language ability. Last, Joe performed ongoing self-reflection throughout his unit, writing weekly reflection entries in a journal and videotaping himself teaching and writing an extensive self-evaluation of the video. After looking at all of the factors taken together, Joe determined that his students did, in fact, learn. The formal assessments and analysis of data provided evidence that most students were able to meet the objectives in the unit; and, the outside and self-evaluations rounded out the evidence that Joe had been effective in his teaching. Looking ahead to the next time he taught the unit, the last thing Joe did was create a chart of what to keep, what to adjust and what to eliminate the next time. He put this in the file package he organized containing all of the materials needed for this unit on pet care.

CONCLUSION

The Georgia Elementary School Foreign Languages Model Program has an appropriate and exemplary curriculum. We have tried to show in Chapter 3 how the curriculum is organized, why it is appropriate and how to use it for a unit of instruction. The sample provided is only one of many excellent units Model Program teachers create. The effective units all have several things in common: they are based directly on the curriculum, they are organized around a theme, they contain vocabulary and structures determined to be appropriate for the students' level, neither too little nor too much; they incorporate content-related activities as part of meaningful communication; they are standards-based; they begin with a goal in mind, the formal assessments, and every activity builds toward student success on these assessments; teachers plan not only for mimic and repetition, but for extended, meaningful use of the language; there is ongoing informal assessment; effort is made to address different multiple intelligences and learning styles; and analysis of the assessment data followed by teacher self-assessment and plans for improvement in the future are part of the ongoing process.

NOTE

1. The website for the Georgia Quality Core Curriculum is continually upgraded and entrance pathways to a particular part of the curriculum may change. At the time of this publication, due to formatting constraints, the webbed curriculum cannot be located through the main standards of the Georgia Quality Core Curriculum but is accessed through the following steps:

   - Enter the website www.glc.k12.ga.us.
   - Click on QCC Standards and Resources.
   - Look for the blue box at left, click on Projects and Programs.
   - Click on the box Languages and International Education.
   - Click on QCC Standards and Resources for Modern and Classical Languages.
   - Scroll to the bottom, click on QCC Standards and Related Resources for Elementary, Middle, and High School.
   - At the top, click on Elementary Foreign Language Curriculum.
   - At the top, click on the grade level desired.
   - To locate the thematic web, click on Grade X Thematic Web.
   - To access the other components of the curriculum for each grade, click on the desired grade level links.

CHAPTER 4

PROGRAM AND STUDENT ASSESSMENT

INTRODUCTION

Georgia's Elementary School Foreign Languages Model Program serves as a model of excellence because its positive effects on student language learning have been assessed and documented. Student language proficiency in listening comprehension and oral fluency skills has been evaluated three times by the Center for Applied Linguistics (CAL) from Washington, DC. Other program assessments include two attitude studies. In the first, the students reported on their attitudes toward studying a foreign language and on what they perceived they could do in the foreign language. In the second, teachers, administrators and parents indicated what their attitudes were toward the Model Program. Finally, a quantitative analysis was conducted comparing the performance of Model Program foreign language students to their peers who did not take a foreign language on the mathematics and reading comprehension sections of the Iowa Tests of Basic Skills. Each of the studies validated the positive effect that foreign language study has for Model Program students. These studies will be described in detail in the following sections.

Early Language Learning: A Model for Success, 69–99
Copyright © 2004 by Information Age Publishing
All rights of reproduction in any form reserved.

PROGRAM EVALUATION

At the end of the 1994-95 school year, at the request of the Georgia Department of Education, the Center for Applied Linguistics conducted a program evaluation of Georgia's Elementary School Foreign Languages Model Program. Adger (1995) found the Model Program to be "regarded in the field of foreign language teaching as a state-of-the-art model" with "implications for a national audience" (p. 1). CAL's evaluation included both quantitative data in the form of a survey and qualitative data derived from site visits. The survey was administered to 54 Model Program teachers and 41 associated school administrators and contact people with a rate of return of 56% for teachers and 68% for administrators. In addition, daylong visits to Model Program sites for each language were conducted. The CAL researchers observed classes, interviewed district and school administrators, Model Program teachers, classroom teachers, parents and the two state directors of the Model Program. The data indicated that the administrators were "very satisfied with the program" and were "willing to work to keep it in their schools and to continually refine it" (p. 3). The teachers indicated "a high level of satisfaction" with the Model Program, with their professional development experiences, with the support they received from their administrators and with their relationships to students and parents. Areas of concern expressed by survey respondents included space, scheduling, teacher supply, late entrants into the program and stable funding. Adger made five recommendations to improve the program: (1) stabilize funding; (2) accommodate newcomers; (3) integrate the Model Program and the regular curriculum; (4) expand student response opportunities in instruction; and (5) advocate for and disseminate the program (Ibid.). Adger concluded by saying, "Georgia's ESFL Model Program is excellent by any measure. Moreover, the fact that continuous renewal of curriculum and professional development are inherent in the program promises that it will continue its high quality" (Ibid.).

Since the program evaluation, several of Adger's recommendations were acted upon by program supervisors and teachers. For instance, as the curriculum was revised and expanded, efforts were made to integrate more of the regular curriculum into the Model Program curriculum. Teachers and schools also addressed the problem of newcomers. In several schools special newcomer classes were formed, and in others teachers offered extra tutoring or classes before or after school to help recent arrivals to the program. The frequent professional development, including a special workshop by Carol M. Saunders Semonsky titled, "Beyond Vocabulary: Elicitation of Extended Language in the Upper Elementary Grades," focused on training teachers to provide more opportunities for student response participation. Funding the Model Program is still problematic. In spite of advocacy campaigns organized by Model Program teachers, parents and students, funding has yet to be stabilized by the Georgia legislature. It is a line item in the annual budget and has been cut several times. Fortunately, to date, the strong advocacy effort has convinced policy makers to add the Model Program funds back into the budget each year that funds were cut.

ASSESSMENT OF
MODEL PROGRAM STUDENT LANGUAGE PROFICIENCY

At the request of the Georgia Department of Education, language researchers from the Center for Applied Linguistics, based in Washington, DC, conducted three separate assessments of the listening comprehension and speaking proficiencies of the Georgia Model Program students.

Assessments performed in 1997, 1998, and 2001 focused mainly on determining the proficiency level of Model Program students in the areas of oral fluency and listening comprehension skills. CAL researchers and Model Program teachers conducted student language proficiency interviews in selected Model Program sites. In order to prepare Model Program teachers for the interviews, training sessions for interviewers and raters were conducted by CAL staff. A schedule was created so that CAL staff and Model Program teachers interviewed as a team at schools other than the teachers' home schools. All interview sessions were both videotaped and audio recorded for cross-verification of assigned ratings by the CAL researchers. The researchers also examined other issues such as whether Model Program students were making progress in their language skills from year to year, how Model Program student language proficiency compared with that of other FLES models, and if longer lengths of study led to greater language proficieny. The three studies will be described below.

Study 1: 1997

In 1997, the Center for Applied Linguistics assessed third grade students using the Student Oral Proficiency Assessment (SOPA). A copy of the SOPA instrument is found in Appendix H. The Student Oral Proficiency Assessment is described as follows:

> The SOPA is composed of four tasks which are set in an interview format. The SOPA interview takes from 10 to 15 minutes to administer with the goal

of guiding the students to the highest level at which they are able to perform in both listening comprehension and oral fluency. For this reason, the SOPA is conducted by two examiners, one primarily for interviewing and the other primarily for rating. The interview is conducted entirely in the target language. Students are evaluated in pairs to facilitate dialogues between them and the examiners and between each other. The focus of the interview is to discover what the students *can* do rather than what they cannot do. The SOPA rating scale is adapted from the first six levels of a nine-level scale from the CAL Oral Proficiency Exam (COPE), designed to assess the listening and speaking skills of fifth and sixth grade students. These scales are based on the proficiency guidelines of the American Council on the Teaching of Foreign Languages (ACTFL). The six levels of the SOPA rating are: *Junior Novice-Low, Junior Novice-Mid, Junior Novice-High, Junior Intermediate-Low, Junior Intermediate-Mid, and Junior Intermediate-High* (Boyson, 1997).

The four tasks students are asked to perform are (1) to manipulate and name small plastic fruits and give their color and number; (2) to respond to informal personal questions and TPR commands; (3) to describe and manipulate house and family colorforms; and (4) to describe a classroom picture and manipulate corresponding classroom objects. The interview ends with a wind-down where the interviewer compliments the students and wishes them a good day (Rhodes & Thompson, 1990).

Third grade students from seven Model Program schools, two schools each offering French, German or Spanish, and one school offering Japanese, were assessed. All 320 students had studied their foreign language for three years and approximately three months for 30 minutes daily. The combined ratings for the four languages in the seven schools are found in Table 4.1. The majority of students ranked at the Junior Novice-Mid and Junior Novice-High levels for both listening comprehension and oral fluency. The CAL study also showed that there was variance among the

Table 4.1. Combined Percentages of Model Program Third Grade Students in Seven Schools According to Listening Comprehension and Oral Fluency on the SOPA Rating Scale in 1997

	Level						
	Jr. Nov-Low	Jr. Nov-Mid	Jr. Nov-High	Jr. Int-Low	Jr. Int-Mid	Jr. Int/High	Totals
Listening Comprehension	6% n (19)	40% n (129)	37% n (120)	16% n (50)	1% n (2)		100% N 320
Oral Fluency	25% n (79)	46% n (147)	26% n (85)	3% n (9)			100% N 320

Source: Boyson (1997).

skills. That students scored higher in listening comprehension than in oral fluency is in keeping both with the program delivery, which emphasizes a great amount of language input from the teacher, and with how young children learn their native language. Boyson, in her analysis, stated that "students are adequately reaching the desired levels of proficiency in their foreign language development. This is one indication that the long-range goal of the program, to produce fluent users of the target languages, is being accomplished" (Boyson, 1997, p. 3).

The number of hours needed on the average for young learners to advance from one level of proficiency to another has not yet been determined (Boyson, 1997). The rate, however, for adult learners at the Foreign Service Institute has been delineated (Liskin-Gasparro, 1982). A motivated adult learner in an immersion setting requires 240 hours of study in French or Spanish or 480 hours of study in German or Japanese to advance from the novice to the intermediate level of proficiency. The Model Program students had approximately 285 contact hours in their foreign language classes. This includes subtracting ten classes per year for school-related activities and standardized testing when no foreign language classes were held. Some of the elementary school foreign language students, who of course were at a lower cognitive level than the adults at the Foreign Service Institute, were still able to rate at Junior Novice-High. If we equate the 285 hours of foreign language contact with a child learning his first language, allowing 10 waking hours per day of contact in the native language, the foreign language students would have had the approximate equivalent of 29 days of contact with the language. In view of this, the progress that the students made in their foreign language proficiency from ages five to eight is remarkable.

Study 2: 1998

In 1998, the Georgia Department of Education again contacted researchers at the Center for Applied Linguistics to assess the language proficiency of Model Program students. There were two stated goals for this assessment: (1) to compare the SOPA ratings of fifth grade students with those of third grade students in the Model Program to determine if students were adequately progressing in their skills, and (2) to compare the proficiency levels of fifth grade students in the Model Program with those of fifth grade students in non-Model Program FLES programs. For this assessment, a version of the Student Oral Proficiency Assessment (SOPA) appropriate for fifth grade students was developed and administered to a random sample of 100 fifth grade students taking one of the four languages offered by the Model Program.

Table 4.2. Comparison in Percentages of Third and Fifth Grade Model Program Students in Listening Comprehension on the SOPA Rating Scale in 1998

Grade	Listening Comprehension						
	Jr. Nov-Low	Jr. Nov-Mid	Jr. Nov-High	Jr. Int-Low	Jr. Int-Mid	Jr. Int-High	Totals
3rd	6% n (19)	40% n (129)	37% n (120)	16% n (50)	1% n (2)		100% N 320
5th		10% n (26)	30% n (81)	23% n (62)	20% n (53)	17% n (46)	100% N 268

Source: Boyson and Thompson (1998).

Table 4.3. Comparison in Percentages of Third and Fifth Grade Model Program Students in Oral Fluency on the SOPA Rating Scale in 1998

Grade	Oral Fluency						
	Jr. Nov-Low	Jr. Nov-Mid	Jr. Nov-High	Jr. Int-Low	Jr. Int-Mid	Jr. Int-High	Totals
3rd	25% n (79)	46% n (147)	26% n (85)	3% n (9)			100% N 320
5th	8% n (20)	28% n (75)	34% n (91)	17% n (46)	13% n (36)		100% N 268

Source: Boyson and Thompson (1998).

The CAL findings, located in Tables 4.2 and 4.3, show that the fifth grade students were progressing in their language skills, with more fifth graders ranking in the higher levels of the proficiency scales than their third grade counterparts. In their Executive Summary, Boyson and Thompson (1998) stated, "Considering that progress in foreign language learning in the classroom takes place gradually, it is evident that the students in the ESFL Model Program are reaching commendable levels of proficiency. Many of the students in the fifth grade comprehend everyday topics and some academic topics at a normal rate of speed in the foreign language. A number of students can converse interactively, using sentence-level speech" (p. 1).

In the comparison of the Model Program and non-Model Program FLES students, the researchers acknowledged that students in both programs were doing well in their foreign language skills. As Tables 4.4 and 4.5 show, fifth grade students in the Model Program outperformed their non-Model Program counterparts by having a greater percentage of students scoring in the higher levels of the SOPA rating scales. According to

Table 4.4. Comparison in Percentages of Model Program and Non-Model Program Fifth Grade Students in Listening Comprehension on the SOPA Rating Scale in 1998

Program Type	Listening Comprehension						
	Jr. Nov-Low	Jr. Nov-Mid	Jr. Nov-High	Jr. Int-Low	Jr. Int-Mid	Jr. Int-High	Totals
MP		10 n (26)	30 n (81)	23 n (62)	20 n (53)	17 n (46)	100% N 268
Non-MP	10 n (12)	26 n (32)	53 n (66)	10 n (12)	1 n (2)		100% N 124

Source: Boyson and Thompson (1998).

Table 4.5. Comparison in Percentages of Model Program and Non-Model Program Fifth Grade Students in Oral Fluency on the SOPA Rating Scale in 1998

Program Type	Oral Fluency						
	Jr. Nov-Low	Jr. Nov-Mid	Jr. Nov-High	Jr. Int-Low	Jr. Int-Mid	Jr. Int-High	Totals
MP	8% n (20)	28% n (75)	34% n (91)	17% n (46)	13% n (36)	0	100% N 268
Non-MP	30% n (37)	52% n (64)	15% n (18)	3% n (4)			100% N 124

Source: Boyson and Thompson (1998).

the researchers, "a substantial portion of students in the ESFL Model Program exceeded expectations in their ability to comprehend and speak the languages they are learning" (Boyson & Thompson, 1998, p. 2).

Study 3: 2001

The third study by the Center for Applied Linguistics had five goals: (1) to determine the proficiency level of Model Program students in kindergarten, third grade and fifth grade; (2) to compare the proficiency levels of the three grades to determine if listening comprehension and oral fluency abilities had increased with additional years of study; (3) to compare language proficiency of Model Program and non-Model Program third and fifth grade students; (4) to compare the 1998 and 2001 SOPA ratings as a means of monitoring program quality and consistency; and (5) to compare the performance of students who had begun their study of their foreign language in kindergarten or first grade with those who had a later start.

The SOPA, described earlier, was administered to a random sample of 189 third grade and 149 fifth grade students of French, German, Japanese, and Spanish. The Early Language Listening and Oral Proficiency Assessment (ELLOPA) was administered to 168 kindergarten students of the same four languages. The ELLOPA is described as "an interactive listening and speaking assessment designed for children ages 4-8, who are learning a foreign or second language in a school setting (Pre-K through Grade 2). Two students at a time participate in a series of five language games where they interact with a puppet that speaks only the foreign language the students are learning" (Thompson & Boyson, 2001, p.5). The tasks are similar to the SOPA tasks but are at a lower level and include singing. For this assessment, the expanded SOPA/COPE Rating Scale was used. Both the SOPA Rating Scale and the ELLOPA Rating Profile (ELLOPA-RP) determine ratings for oral fluency, including grammar and vocabulary, and for listening comprehension. In addition to the interviews, oral fluency and listening comprehension levels of the students were determined by using teacher ratings of students based on overall classroom performance and student self-assessment instruments. The SOPA Self-Assessment (SSA) consists of statements that describe the ability to perform speaking or listening tasks in the target language. A 4-level Lickert scale is used, ranging from "Yes" to "Not Yet" and students estimate their ability in each area. The Early Language Learner Self-Assessment (ELLSSA), used with the kindergarten children, has 18 pictures representing topics and functions that are typically taught in the early years of foreign language instruction. Students are asked to color in one happy face if they "don't know this yet," two happy faces if they "know a little about this," and three happy faces if they "know this" (Thompson & Boyson, 2001, pp 6-7).

The analysis of the performance of the kindergarten students, who had been studying their target language for seven months, showed that most students rated in the Junior Novice-Low and Junior Novice-Mid range for speaking, including oral fluency, grammar and vocabulary. For listening comprehension and communication strategies, these young students rated mostly in the Junior Novice-Mid range. Teacher ratings of these same students based on their classroom work was at the Junior Novice-Low range for oral fluency and grammar, and between Junior Novice-Mid and Junior Novice-High for listening comprehension, vocabulary and communication strategies. This slightly higher estimate of student ability by the teachers may be a result of their taking into account the day in and day out performance of the students and the fact that students may perform better in their own classrooms than in a formal interview with strangers. In the ELLSSA self-report, 89-96% of students perceived that they knew or knew a little about such topics as numbers, weather, family, greetings, colors, body parts, their name, asking how you are and animals. They indicated less confidence in their proficiency when talking about school, holidays, food, seasons, clothes and expressing likes and dislikes (Thompson & Boyson, 2001). Some of these latter topics are only briefly addressed or not addressed at all in kindergarten. For instance, there are only five school items presented in the kindergarten curriculum and seasons are not addressed until first grade (Georgia Department of Education, 2002b). The researchers from the Center for Applied Linguistics summed up the performance of kindergarten students in the Model Program by stating, "Kindergarten ELLOPA ratings and ELLOPA-RP teacher ratings of their students using the ELLOPA-RP indicate commendable levels of proficiency that are often not achieved by students with less than a year of foreign language study" (Thompson & Boyson, 2001, p. 50).

The results of the third grade students, seen in Table 4.6, ranged from Junior Novice-Low to Junior Intermediate-High with most students rating between Junior Novice-Mid and Junior Novice-High. Students rated highest in listening comprehension, followed by oral fluency, vocabulary and grammar. When looking at the languages individually, Spanish learners received the highest ratings, followed by German, French, and Japanese. Across all languages, students showed the least variation in listening comprehension with average scores ranging between Junior Novice-Mid and Junior Intermediate-Low. The average teacher ratings for oral fluency, vocabulary and grammar were between Junior Novice-High and Junior Intermediate-Mid for French, German, and Spanish. For listening comprehension, average teacher ratings were between Junior Intermedi-

Table 4.6. Percentages by Level for SOPA Ratings of Third Grade Model Program Students in 2001

	Jr. Nov-Low	Jr. Nov-Mid	Jr. Nov-High	Jr. Int-Low	Jr. Int-Mid	Jr. Int-High	Totals
Oral Fluency	13.2 n (25)	33.3 n (61)	28 n (53)	20.6 n (39)	5.8 n (11)		100% N 189
Grammar	20.1 n (38)	31.2 n (59)	28.6 n (54)	17.5 n (33)	2.6 n (5)		100% N 189
Vocabulary	10.1 n (19)	40.2 n (76)	30.7 n (58)	15.9 n (30)	3.2 n (6)		100% N 189
Listening Comprehension		24.9 n (47)	32.8 n (62)	24.9 n (47)	15.3 n (29)	2.1 n (4)	100% N 189

Source: Thompson and Boyson (2001, p. 23).

ate-Mid and Junior Intermediate-High for the same languages. Japanese students consistently received lower ratings in each skill area, reflecting the fact that Japanese takes more time to learn (Lisken-Gasparro, 1982). CAL determined, "Results confirm that third grade students in the ESFL Model Program are making steady progress in learning languages based on the overall averages from the SOPA ratings, the teacher ratings and the student self-assessment (SSA). The increases in scores between kindergarten and third grade for both ELLOPA and SOPA interviews and for the teachers' ratings are statistically significant ($p < .05$)" (Thompson & Boyson, p. 51).

Most third grade students, in their SSA self-report, indicated that they could count to ten or higher, greet someone and say their name, follow simple command instructions, say the names and ages of their family members, ask someone what his/her name is, give simple command instructions, describe self and others, talk about the weather and identify classroom objects. Most students indicated that they only had "a little" ability to make complete sentences, describe a picture on a familiar topic, talk about their hobbies, tell what they study in school, talk about things in the past or retell a story. The topics in which the students perceived they could do well are emphasized more in the thematic units of the Georgia Quality Core Curriculum than those functions in which students indicated they had a lesser degree of proficiency. In comparison with students in traditional FLES programs that meet three days a week, Model Program students fared better. According to CAL research, traditional FLES students "are generally unable to perform a number of the language functions listed on the SSA . . . Model Program students responded that they could accomplish all of the functions to a certain degree" (Thompson & Boyson, 2001, p. 51).

As seen in Table 4.7, the fifth grade students ranged from Junior Novice-Low to Junior Advanced-High, with most students falling into the Junior Novice-High and Junior Intermediate-Low ranges. Ratings were higher in listening comprehension than for the other skills, reflecting similar findings in kindergarten and third grade. Fifteen students of French or German were able to rate in the Junior Advanced categories, while Junior Intermediate-Mid was the highest rating for students of Japanese or Spanish. It is important to remember that *all* students at Model Program schools, including those with special needs and those with limited English proficiency, participate in the language program, as well as students who may have the opportunity to use the language outside the classroom. For the teacher assessments of student proficiency, the average ratings for oral fluency, vocabulary and listening comprehension were between Junior Intermediate-Low and Junior Intermediate-Mid, and the average ratings for grammar were between Junior Novice-High and Jun-

Table 4.7. Percentages by Level for SOPA Ratings of Fifth Grade Model Program Students in 2001

	Jr. Nov- Low	Jr. Nov- Mid	Jr. Nov- High	Jr. Int- Low	Jr. Int- Mid	Jr. Int- High	Jr. Adv- Low	Jr. Adv- Mid	Jr. Adv- High	Totals
Oral Fluency	1.3 n (2)	15.4 n (23)	25.5 n (38)	26.8 n (40)	17.4 n (26)	10.7 n (16)	2.7 n (4)			100% N 149
Grammar	1.3 n (2)	19.5 n (29)	28.2 n (42)	30.2 n (45)	16.8 n (25)	3.4 n (5)			0.7% n (1)	100% N 149
Vocabulary	0.7 n (1)	18.1 n (27)	36.2 n (54)	16.8 n (25)	18.8 n (28)	8.1 n (12)	0.7 n (1)		0.7% n (1)	100% N 149
Listening Comp.		6.7 n (10)	25.5 n (38)	22.8 n (34)	18.8 n (28)	20.8 n (31)	3.4 n (5)	1.3 n (2)	0.7 n (1)	100% N 149

Source: Thompson and Boyson (2001, p. 37).

ior Intermediate-Low. The teachers' assessments of their students' abilities matched those of the SOPA assessments in grammar and were slightly higher for the other areas.

For the Student Self-Assessment of language proficiencies, more than 50% of students responded "Yes" that they could talk about 11 out of 15 topic areas. The one language function that slightly more than half of the students reported they were just starting to do was to retell a story or fairytale. The other areas where students felt less confident included talking about things in the past, describing a picture and talking about subjects studied in school. All of the areas the students felt they were just beginning to be able to do require fairly complex language skills such as describing and using past tense(s). It is interesting to note that for the item addressing the ability to talk about things that happened in the past, the highest average score in this category was received by students of Japanese and the lowest by students of Spanish. The familiarity or non-familiarity of students with certain functions depends on when the topics are presented in the curriculum and how much attention and practice the individual teachers provide for each function.

The CAL researchers again confirmed that students were making steady progress in their language skills. CAL stated, "This evidence of progress in speaking and listening abilities was found to be statistically significant ($p < .05$) between grades in all skill areas: oral proficiency, grammar, vocabulary and listening comprehension" (Thompson & Boyson, 2001, p. 53).

The third research goal compared third grade and fifth grade Model Program students with those enrolled in traditional FLES programs. There was a difference in the amount of time devoted to foreign language

Table 4.8. Means and Standard Deviations of SOPA Ratings for Oral Fluency and Listening Comprehension for Third Grade Students in the Model Program and a Traditional FLES Program

	Model Program Third Grade N (189)	Traditional FLES Third Grade N (30)
Oral Fluency	M 2.74 SD 1.11	M 1.57 SD .57
Listening Comprehension	M 3.37 SD 1.08	M 2.47 SD .63

Source: Thompson and Boyson (2001, p. 54).

Table 4.9. Means and Standard Deviations of SOPA Ratings for Oral Fluency and Listening Comprehension for Fifth Grade Students in the Model Program and a Traditional FLES Program

	Model Program Fifth Grade N (149)	Traditional FLES Fifth Grade N (60)
Oral Fluency	M 3.87 SD 1.35	M 1.48 SD .62
Listening Comprehension	M 4.40 SD 1.44	M 2.19 SD .72

Source: Thompson and Boyson (2001, p. 54).

study, with the third grade FLES students receiving instruction 30 minutes a day, three days per week and the fifth grade students receiving 20 minutes a day, two days a week. The Model Program students, in keeping with the program's guidelines, received their foreign language instruction 30 minutes per day, five days per week. The averages of the SOPA ratings for listening comprehension and oral fluency for both groups can be seen in Tables 4.8 and 4.9. As in 1998, the Model Program students had higher levels of language proficiency than did the students in other FLES delivery models. For both the third grade and fifth grade students, CAL determined that the SOPA ratings indicated "commendable levels of proficiency that are often not achieved in other language programs" (Thompson & Boyson, 2001, pp. 53, 54).

The CAL researchers performed two final comparisons. The first was between 2001 SOPA ratings for third and fifth grade Model Program students and previous SOPA ratings for Model Program students in these two grades. (Since 2001 was the first time kindergarten students had been assessed, no comparison was possible for this grade level.) While direct comparisons are difficult to analyze because different schools and different students participated in each assessment, the comparison showed that student proficiency was higher in 2001. CAL named some factors that may have contributed to the better performance of third and fifth graders in 2001, among them, "fine-tuning of the ESFL Model Program in areas such as curriculum revision and professional development, and the positive effects of previous performance assessments" (Thompson & Boyson, 2001, p. 55). This finding by CAL demonstrated that the Model Program was maintaining and improving its quality. The last comparison CAL researchers performed was of students who had participated in the Model Program since kindergarten or first grade with students who came into the program at a later grade level. The comparison determined that students in both third and fifth grade who had the longer length of study outperformed newer arrivals.

In concluding remarks, the CAL report reconfirmed the excellence of the Georgia Elementary School Foreign Languages Model Program. According to the Center for Applied Linguistics researchers, the Georgia students were making "commendable progress in acquiring a foreign language" and the Georgia student ratings were "higher than any known average ELLOPA-SOPA ratings in other foreign language elementary programs in the United States" (Thompson & Boyson, 2001, p. 58).[1]

The empirical analyses of the language ability of Model Program students showed that the program was working on many levels. Student speaking and listening skills met or exceeded expectations at the three grade levels tested: kindergarten, third grade and fifth grade. Students who remained in the program over time improved their proficiency as they progressed through the program. And, in two comparisons with non-Model Program FLES students, the Model Program foreign language students outperformed the students enrolled in other delivery models. Decision makers, school administrators, teachers, parents and the students themselves have every reason to be proud of the success of this early foreign language program.

MODEL PROGRAM STUDENT ACHIEVEMENT ON THE IOWA TESTS OF BASIC SKILLS

Students in the Model Program are clearly progressing in their foreign language skills. Still, some administrators, classroom teachers and parents have raised objections to scheduling foreign language study for 30 minutes a day for fear that other important "basic skills" will suffer. It is an area of concern and, sometimes, annoyance to foreign language teachers that foreign language proficiency is not valued in and of itself. Foreign language teachers, unlike many of their fellow academic colleagues, may have to justify the worthiness of their program based on the fact that it helps performance or is not detrimental to academic achievement in other areas. The importance of the study of mathematics is never questioned because the end result, mathematical knowledge, is valued. Nor are math teachers required to cite research that math is worthy of inclusion in the curriculum because it benefits English, science or social studies skills. But foreign language teachers, especially at the elementary school level, are frequently asked whether taking a foreign language will help math or language arts skills.

While research shows that beginning foreign language study early and extending it over a long sequence is best, it is hard to convince districts that their investment in time and money in foreign language programs will be worth it. ACTFL's estimate of how long it takes students to progress from novice to intermediate ability in a foreign language is between 3 and 6 years (Duncan & Swender, 1998). It is important to note that those subjects truly valued as part of the necessary basic curriculum for students begin in kindergarten and continue throughout high school. Since foreign language proficiency is important for American students in order to compete on an international level, it merits a place in an extended articulated sequence. Foreign language educators, parents and students, and businessmen may recognize that developing accomplished speakers of a foreign language is a worthy goal in itself, but many administrators balk at funding programs whose results may not be immediately evident. They look therefore to other evidentiary support that will help them justify funding and scheduling the foreign language program. The area that many administrators view as an important factor in their rationale to offer foreign languages is that taking a foreign language helps students do well in other skill areas, especially if this is reflected on standardized tests. It is with this end in mind that a body of research has appeared linking foreign language study to increased ability in other academic areas.

Research on Foreign Language Study and Academic Achievement

Several researchers of early FLES models were interested in showing that FLES was not detrimental to academic achievement (Geigle, 1957; Johnson, Ellison, & Flores, 1963; Lopato, 1963). Lopato (1963) compared the achievement on the Stanford Achievement Test of third grade students enrolled in ALM French for fifteen minutes a day to third grade students not enrolled in FLES. Comparisons between the pretest and the post-test showed significant differences in favor of the French students in spelling and arithmetic at one school, but only in arithmetic at the other school. Out of eight statistical tests, three were statistically significant. Lopato concluded that exposure to FLES was not detrimental to academic performance, basing her contention on the fact that in seven out of eight instances the French group showed greater mean achievement. Geigle (1957) also compared achievement of FLES French students and non-FLES students. He found that the FLES fourth graders showed equivalent achievement to non-FLES students in reading, arithmetic, language usage, and spelling. Research by Vollmer (1962) found that FLES students had high school grades that were 10% higher than non-FLES students.

Johnson et al. (1963) evaluated the extensive (3 year) elementary Spanish program initiated by the University of Illinois. This program offered daily instruction in Spanish, which required shortening the instructional periods of other academic subjects. The research compared time taken from social studies, arithmetic or language arts. The researchers found that the time deleted from these academic areas did not reduce the extent of average gain in student achievement on the Iowa Tests of Basic Skills. The FLES and non-FLES groups showed no difference in the areas of language skills, work study skills and arithmetic, but the FLES group showed a significant gain in scores over the other group in the areas of reading vocabulary and reading comprehension.

Leino and Haak (1963) found similar results when they compared students in three grades (fourth, fifth, and sixth) in St. Paul, Minnesota. The students were exposed to Spanish for fifteen minutes a day. The students watched a Spanish television show aimed at teaching the language to young learners three times a week accompanied by twice-weekly work with audiotapes. The classroom teachers had a weekly "preview" presentation designed especially for them, and they also received workbooks and other written support material to help them reinforce the program. The researchers used the ITBS, the Stanford Social Studies Test, and the Otis Beta Intelligence Test to compare language to non-language groups. The results showed that the experimental group experienced no detrimental effect from the reduction of class time in language, social studies or arithmetic. Leino and Haak also reached the conclusion that "measured intelligence is positively correlated with measured achievement in the learning of Spanish .... so students of low intelligence would be better off concentrating on the basic skills of reading, spelling, writing and arithmetic" (p. 29). Later research by Tabor (1987) and Garfinkel and Tabor (1991) refuted this idea. Gordon, Engar, and Shupe (1963) evaluated a program which offered Russian by means of television to elementary students with above average (115+) IQs. They found that students learning Russian performed better in grades 4-6 in science and social studies and students performed better in arithmetic and spelling in grades 5-7. These researchers also found that students in the upper range of IQ who had FLES exhibited better emotional control, more leadership and more self-initiated drive than the non-FLES group. Landry (1974) found that students who had taken a foreign language since the first grade scored higher on a measure of divergent thinking skills than the non-FLES students.

Elementary school immersion programs have been extensively studied by researchers associated with the St. Lambert Project outside of Montreal (Lambert & Tucker, 1972; Lambert, Tucker, & d'Anglejan, 1965). The researchers conducted a longitudinal study of two groups of English-speaking children who participated in a partial immersion (60% of class day taught in French) program in grades K-4. They were matched with English speakers who were taught their academics in English, and the results in several areas were compared and analyzed at the end of each year. Lambert et al. (1965) found,

> After five years, we are satisfied that the experimental program has resulted in no native language or subject matter (i.e., arithmetic) deficit or retardation of any sort, nor is there any cognitive retardation attributable to participation in the program. In fact, the Experimental pupils appear to be able to read, write, speak, understand, and use English as competently as youngsters instructed in the conventional manner via English. During the same period of time and with no apparent personal or academic costs, the children have developed a competence in reading, writing, speaking and understanding French that English pupils following a traditional French-As-A-Second-Language program for the same number of years could never match (p.152).

Similar analyses of immersion programs in the United States (Cohen, 1974) showed that, while at first immersion students in kindergarten lagged behind their peers taught in English, by the end of the second year, there was no difference between the two groups on a test of English morphology and that the immersion students did significantly better on a test of English storytelling. The equal or greater performance of immersion over non immersion students is confirmed by several other researchers, notably Lebach (1974), and Rhodes et al. (1981).

Researchers continued to be interested in the relationship of the study of a foreign language to academic achievement in other areas. Hakuta (1984) found that bilingual students demonstrated greater cognitive flexibility. Both Eddy (1981) and Cooper (1987) conducted research to determine the effect of language study on students' verbal scores on the Scholastic Aptitude Test (SAT). Eddy did a stepwise multiple regression and found that, when verbal ability was controlled, students who studied language for longer periods of time did better on various sub-tests and on the SAT-verbal as a whole than students who studied less foreign language. He also found that higher grades in foreign language classes increased the effect of foreign language study on SAT scores, particularly on the reading and vocabulary sub-tests. Eddy's control group was very small ($N = 7$).

In 1987, Cooper replicated Eddy's study, but he was able to make a direct comparison between the FL and NFL groups. Using scores from the California Achievement Test as a covariate to control for verbal ability and the SAT-verbal as the dependent variable, Cooper found that there were significant ($p < .0001$) differences in favor of the FL students.

Like Eddy, Cooper was able to show that, for students who completed full years of study in their foreign language, length of study in the foreign language was closely linked to superior SAT-verbal scores. Another interesting finding by Cooper was that the language studied also made a difference in scores. German students achieved the highest SAT-verbal scores, followed by French and Latin, and, finally, Spanish. Cooper pointed out several learning strategies that students learn from a conscientious foreign language teacher which may reinforce skills needed to do well on the SAT-verbal. Among these strategies were: (1) learning vocabulary in context; (2) developing a sensitivity for nuance in the meaning of words; (3) using contextual cues to guess at the meaning of unknown words in a passage; and (4) reading a text with care and special attention to thematic development, style, and the author's stance to his material (Cooper, 1987, p. 386).

In 1991, Garfinkel and Tabor compared elementary students with a minimum introduction to Spanish in the third and fourth grades (20 minutes twice a week for nine weeks) to those students who opted to extend their study of Spanish into the fifth or sixth grade (25 minutes sessions before or after school, two or three times a week). They further divided the students into low, medium and high intelligence groups to test for differences in achievement of the various intelligence levels. They found that, overall, extending the study of Spanish did not make a significant difference in reading ability. They did find, however, that for the low ability group, there were significant differences in sixth grade reading achievement. They implied that reading scores should not be used as a criterion for determining who should or should not take a foreign language. Research on immersion programs seems to support Garfinkel and Tabor's claims that IQ should not be used to eliminate students from foreign language study. Bruck, Lambert, and Tucker (1979) found that students whose IQs were below average or who had learning disabilities were not at any more of a disadvantage in immersion programs than they were in all-English programs.

One of the most extensive comparisons of the effects of achievement to early foreign language study was conducted by Rafferty in 1986. She used a sample of $N = 13,500$. She evaluated students in grades three, four, and five who had been exposed to the daily study of French through Louisiana's CODOFIL (Committee of the Development of French In Louisiana) Program. Louisiana mandated that all elementary students in Louisiana study French. The state had an ambitious program, with cooperation from the French government, that included importing teachers from target countries to teach some of the classes. It prohibited the use of exploratory foreign language classes and said that "foreign languages in grades 4 through 8 shall be taught in the subject area(s) designated by the local School board" (Louisiana State Department of Education, 1993, p. 3). The state made a special effort to recruit "foreign associate teachers" who were certified teachers in their own countries and were granted interim certification while working in Louisiana. Rafferty used the Louisiana Basic Skills Test, a criterion-referenced instrument designed to measure core curriculum mastery in language arts and math, as her dependent variable. She performed a three-level ANCOVA (treatment versus nontreatment; math and language arts; and, race, sex, and grade). Rafferty's results were mixed. She found that significant differences appeared across all grades in language arts, with foreign language students scoring higher than non-foreign language students (the advantage was more than doubled in favor of the foreign language group by the fifth grade); but for math there was no main effect of second language study. She did find that, although the foreign language students showed some disadvantage on the math test in fourth grade, by fifth grade they performed better than the non-foreign language students.

Georgia's Elementary School Foreign Languages Model Program Students and Academic Achievement

In 1998, Saunders looked at the effect that taking a foreign language as part of the Model Program design had on student performance on a test of basic skills. She compared scores on the mathematics and reading comprehension subtests of the Iowa Tests of Basic Skills (ITBS) of Model Program students with those of their peers from the same school not enrolled in foreign language study. The Georgia Model Program has an institutional cycle design in which the program is begun in kindergarten and one grade level is added in each subsequent year. In this design, when the first Model Program students were in third grade, their peers from the same school in the fourth grade had not taken a foreign language. Saunders compared the ITBS scores of students in the third grade during the

1994-95 school year, none of whom took a foreign language, to students from the same school who were in the third grade during the 1995-96 school year, all of whom took a foreign language.

To remedy the effect that the interdependence of students in classes from the same schools may have on the power, Saunders used a blocking design. In this design, instead of comparing individual students to one another, researchers group students into blocks or cells, add up the means for all students in the block and use this group mean as the basis for comparison. The object of blocking is to create groups that have greater homogeneity among measures within levels of the blocking variable. According to Stevens (1990), blocking adds to the power and helps counteract the fact that the sample was not randomly chosen. In Saunders' study, the entire foreign language (FL) and non-foreign language (non-FL) third-grade classes in participating schools were considered the subjects rather than individual students within each of these classes. The group means for each school was the unit of analysis. Saunders checked for systematic change taking place in the nature of the students, the teachers, or school curriculum between the 1994-1995 and 1995-1996 school years and eliminated any schools where systematic change had occurred. The remaining 18 schools in the sample had all offered a foreign language for three or four years under the Model Program design and were assumed to be generally equated. Three of the schools offered French, three offered Japanese, two offered German and ten offered Spanish. The schools were spread out over the state with ten schools located in north Georgia, three in metro Atlanta, and five in south Georgia.

There have been several forms of the ITBS developed over the years; in both years of the research, 1995 and 1996, Georgia students were administered form M. The Riverside Publishers Catalog (Riverside Publishing, 1996b) offers a brief description of the various tests. The Reading Comprehension Test has cross-content selections, some drawn from social studies and science. The questions measure students' abilities to infer meaning and interpret what they have read, and the catalog states, "critical thinking and interpretive questions are used at every level of the tests" (p. 8). The Mathematics subtests include data interpretation that uses charts and graphs to assess students' ability to understand data, make inferences, analyze and predict. There are word problems that "encourage mathematical connections across content areas" and are "presented in realistic contexts" (p. 8). Saunders' study used the national percentile rank scores because these were the scores that the State of Georgia provided to the public in its annual report on the state of Georgia schools, the *Georgia Public Education 1995-96 Report Cards* (Georgia Department of Education, 1996). Percentile ranks indicate the relative standing of a stu-

Table 4.10. Statistical Analysis of FL and Non-FL Student Performance on the ITBS

Variable	n	df	M	SD	t
ITBS Math	18	17	3.8333	8.4592	1.9926*
ITBS Reading	18	17	.7222	8.2019	.3736

*$p < .05$.
Source: Saunders (1998).

dent in comparison to other students and tell the percent of students in a norm group who obtain lower scores. Thus, a score of 54 means that a particular student scored better than 54% of students in the norm group who took the test.

For the statistical analyses, Saunders compared 18 blocks each of the FL students and the non-FL students. The composite school scores for each year formed the blocks. The dependent variables were the scores on the mathematics subtest and reading comprehension subtest, and the independent variable for each analysis was participation or non-participation in the Georgia Elementary School Foreign Languages Model Program. A dependent sample pre-treatment/post-treatment t-test was performed. Table 4.10 shows the results of Saunders' statistical analysis.

The statistical analysis showed that students taking a foreign language in the elementary school under the Model Program design had higher scores on the mathematics subtests of the Iowa Tests of Basic Skills than did their peers from the same schools who did not take a foreign language. For the reading comprehension subtests, the foreign language students did not have statistically significantly higher scores than their peers who did not take a foreign language.

The findings of the statistical analysis may seem paradoxical at first. The original question of whether taking a foreign language in the elementary school leads to increased scores on standardized tests in basic skills areas seems to be answered both "yes" and "no." Results show that taking a foreign language did improve standardized scores in math but that there was not compelling evidence for the improvement in reading. Why would this be so?

According to Saunders, the answer may lie in the Model Program curriculum itself. The curriculum emphasizes content-related objectives. Although many subject areas are incorporated into foreign language classes, for the two areas under statistical consideration, mathematics and reading, mathematics receives much more emphasis in the foreign language curriculum for grades K-3 than does reading comprehension. Table 4.11 enumerates the mathematics content-related progress indica-

Table 4.11. Math-related Progress Indicators from the Model Program Curriculum

Grade		Math-related Progress Indicators from the Model Program Curriculum
K	K-14:	Students will recognize and count the numbers 0 to 31.
	K-15:	Students will solve simple mathematical problems dealing with addition using numbers 1-10.
1st	1.27:	Students will identify and name numbers 0 to 100.
	1.28:	Students will count by 10s from 0 to 100.
	1.29:	Students will add and subtract using single digits.
	1.30:	Students will recognize and use ordinal numbers first through fifth.
	1.32:	Students will measure objects using nonstandard units.
	1.34:	Students will recognize, describe, and classify objects by shape, color, and size. (a graphing activity)
2nd	2.38:	Students will recognize and use currency from target language countries.
3rd	3.13:	Students will tell time to the hour, half hour, quarter hour, an in digital format.
	3.19:	Students will count, identify, and manipulate numerals 0-100 and count by hundreds to one thousand.
	3.21:	Students will estimate and measure length of classroom objects using the metric system.
	3.22:	Students will estimate and measure temperature in Celsius and Fahrenheit.
	3.24:	Students will compose and describe his weekly schedule using time to the hour, half hour and quarter hour.

Source: Georgia Department of Education, Curriculum Services (1996).

Table 4.12. Reading-related Progress Indicators from the Model Program Curriculum

Grade		Reading-related Progress Indicators from the Model Program Curriculum
K	K-25:	Students will be introduced to selected short narratives, fairy and folk tales, traditional rhymes and songs from the target culture.
1st	1.54:	Students will be introduced to selected short narratives, fairy and folk tales from the target language.
2nd	(None)	
3rd	3.11:	Students will contrast positive and negative character traits and invent an ideal friend.
	3.26:	Students will describe and construct a book about an annual school-wide event.
	3.29:	Students will organize letters and target language vocabulary in alphabetical order.
	3.55:	Students will list famous fairy tales of the target culture.
	3.56:	Students will identify five literary components of a fairy tale.
	3.57:	Students will give the main idea and retell a fairy tale from the target culture.
	3.58:	Students will compare and contrast fairy tales from the United States and the target culture.

Source: Georgia Department of Education, Curriculum Services (1996).

tors from the Model Program Curriculum for grades K-3, and Table 4.12 lists the reading comprehension progress indicators. There are 14 mathematics-related indicators versus nine reading-related indicators for grades K-3. For grades K-2, there are only two reading indicators versus nine mathematics indicators. It is not really until the third grade that Model Program teachers begin to emphasize reading-related skills. Kindergarten and first-grade foreign language students are just "introduced" to various literary selections, usually fairy tales or big books. Actual reading and word recognition is not mentioned until third grade. The students, who took the ITBS in the spring of third grade, had not had a full year of exposure to reading comprehension objectives. Furthermore, the amount of exposure may have varied according to the number and type of reading objectives individual teachers chose to incorporate into their foreign language classes. Some may have emphasized reading to a great extent, others to a lesser degree.

There is much more emphasis on math progress indicators, and it occurs earlier and more consistently. In first grade, for example, there are six math progress indicators versus one in reading. The first-grade progress indicators include counting by tens, addition and subtraction, use of ordinal numbers, estimating, measuring and classifying. The Model Program students are not just to identify the numbers in their foreign language, they are *to use* numbers in various meaningful manipulations. In a student questionnaire, discussed at length in the next section, 87% of Model Program students responded positively that they could use numbers in their foreign language. The functional use of numbers in the foreign language is stressed at all grade levels, with concepts being recycled and reinforced from year to year.

Why not incorporate reading comprehension progress indicators earlier in the Model Program curriculum? Later exposure to reading is in accordance with second language acquisition theory. Experts (Curtain & Pesola, 1994; Krashen, 1987; Krashen & Terrell, 1983) advocate that listening comprehension should receive the most initial emphasis when learning a foreign language, followed by speaking. Typically, reading and writing the foreign language, while still included, are not as greatly emphasized at the beginning of foreign language study as are listening and speaking.

In her conclusion, Saunders (1998) discussed the implications of studying a foreign language within the context of a content-related curriculum such as that of the Model Program. She stated,

> The research has shown that studying a foreign language in the elementary school under a content-related foreign language curriculum does not interfere with basic skills and may actually help improve scores on standardized

tests. The statistical analysis adds to the body of evidence that time taken from other subjects to make room for the study of a foreign language is not detrimental to basic skills. Indeed, if the foreign language class has a content-related component, taking a foreign language may even help improve scores on standardized tests of basic skills (p. 165).

STUDENT ATTITUDE QUESTIONNAIRE

In 1998, Saunders administered an attitude questionnaire to 822 Model Program students in the fourth grade and found that the students exhibited positive attitudes both toward studying a foreign language and toward interacting with the target cultures. They self-reported a high ability in most of the language skills and indicated that content-related instruction was included in their foreign language class. The results of this questionnaire will be discussed below.

Affect and attitudes have shown to play important roles in foreign language learning. Gardner and others (Gardner, 1985; Gardner & Lambert, 1959; Gardner & Smythe, 1974) developed a socio-educational hypothesis about second language learning. This hypothesis says that attitudes and motivation can affect achievement and that, in turn, achievement in a foreign language can affect attitudes and motivations (Branam, 1997). Gardner defined various aspects of motivation. The first was internal motivation, reflecting the students' attitudes toward native speakers, interest in foreign languages and their desire to integrate into the foreign language community. The second was external motivation, demonstrating a desire to learn a language for practical reasons, such as usefulness in a future career. The third was goal focus motivation, including motivational intensity, desire to learn a specific foreign language and attitudes toward learning foreign languages. Empirical studies (Brustall, 1970; Ely, 1986; Gardner & Lambert, 1959, 1972) have shown that positive attitudes and high motivation are linked both to the desire to study a foreign language and to the ability to do well in that language. Other research (Reistra & Johnson, 1964; Handcock, Lipton, & Baslaw, 1976) indicated that students studying a foreign language in the elementary school had more accepting attitudes toward target language speakers, and toward studying a foreign language in general.

While several student questionnaires have been developed to aid in program evaluation and in determining student attitudes (Barr-Harrington, 1993; The Center for Applied Linguistics, 1988; Gardner & Smythe, 1981; Heining-Boyton, 1991), topics that were of interest to Saunders were not all addressed in these questionnaires. She therefore developed an original questionnaire aimed at answering her individual questions about the Model Program and the perceptions of its students. The questionnaire, a copy of which is found in Appendix I, included questions addressing four broad areas. The questions were:

1. Do the students perceive that they benefit from studying a foreign language? Questions in this category reflect Gardner's concept of external motivation.
2. Do the students have positive attitudes toward foreign languages and the people who speak the foreign language they are studying? Questions in this category reflected Gardner's internal motivation and goal focus categories.
3. What foreign language skills do the students indicate they have? The responses to these questions were used for comparison with the SOPA language proficiency assessments performed by the Center for Applied Linguistics.
4. What content areas do the students indicate they have studied in their foreign language class? Responses to these questions helped determine if the Model Program teachers were implementing the program's goal of incorporating content-related instruction (Saunders, 1998, pp. 84-85).

Saunders formulated items aimed at answering these four questions. A summary of all 25 individual questions grouped under the broad questions they address is found in Table 4.13. The students responded to each item by filling in a pictorial scale. A smiling face stood for "yes," a neutral face stood for "sometimes" and a frowning face stood for "no." For certain negatively worded items, such as "The activities in my FL class are dull," a frowning face answer indicated a positive attitude. These negatively worded items were numbers 2, 3, 5, 17, 23, 24. In figuring the percentage of positive and negative attitudes, for these six items, a frowning face counted as a positive answer.

The overall subject pool for the student-participant questionnaire was composed of Model Program students in the fourth grade. Teachers eliminated students who had entered the program after second grade from participating in the questionnaire. Students in 26 fourth-grade Model Program classes from 14 schools responded to the Student-Participant Questionnaire. The response rate to the questionnaire was 69.7%. There were a total of 822 questionnaire respondents: 192 in French, 56 in German, 81 in Japanese, and 493 in Spanish. Since Spanish was offered in more schools, most respondents were from fourth grade Spanish classes. There were 399 respondents from the North Georgia area, 226 from South Georgia and 197 from schools in metropolitan Atlanta.

Table 4.13. Responses to Student Attitude and Ability Questionnaire

Question	Item	Yes	Sometimes	No	Totals
1. Do Model Program students think that they will benefit from taking a foreign language?	15. My FL Class can help me understand my other subjects.	42% n (345)	32% n (259)	26% n (213)	100% N 817
	25. Learning my FL can help me in my job or in school.	76% n (626)	14% n (117)	9% n (74)	100% N 817
2A. Do MP students have positive attitudes towards their FL class?	1. I like my FL class.	69% n (565)	27% n (220)	4% n (36)	100% N 821
	2. My FL class is boring	12% n (104)	33% n (278)	53% n (437)	100% N 819
	5. The activities in my FL class are dull.	6% n (49)	26% n (208)	68% n (559)	100% N 816
	14. I have fun in my FL class.	64% n (526)	27% n (224)	7% n (55)	100% N 805
2B. Do MP students have a positive attitude towards the people and countries where their FL is spoken?	18. I would like to meet someone from a country where they speak my FL.	76% n (621)	10% n (82)	14% n (117)	100% N 820
	19. I would like to visit a country where they speak my FL.	66% n (543)	15% n (121)	19% n (152)	100% N 816
2C. Do MP students have a positive attitude towards FL study?	9. I am happy to learn my FL.	78% n (643)	15% n (123)	7% n (54)	100% N 820
	16. I want to continue to learn my FL.	73% n (601)	14% n (111)	13% n (107)	100% N 819
	17. I have no interest in taking another FL one day.	35% n (285)	18% n (146)	47% n (385)	100% N 816
	20. I feel special because I can study my FL.	62% n (510)	23% n (188)	15% n (120)	100% N 818

(continued)

Table 4.13. Continued

Question	Item	Yes	Sometimes	No	Totals
	21. Learning my FL is important.	68% n (554)	22% n (182)	10% n (82)	100% N 818
	23. My FL is difficult to learn.	19% n (158)	37% n (299)	43% n (357)	100% N 814
	24. I would be afraid to speak to a person who speaks my FL.	25% n (207)	19% n (152)	56% n (460)	100% N 819
3. Do MP students indicate they have language skills?	6. I can speak some sentences in my FL.	69% n (567)	20% n (168)	10% n (78)	100% N 813
	7. I can read some sentences in my FL.	63% n (515)	29% n (242)	8% n (65)	100% N 822
	8. I can write some words or sentences in my FL.	71% n (584)	19% n (153)	10% n (83)	100% N 820
	4. I understand my teacher when she speaks the FL.	33% n (268)	56% n (458)	11% n (94)	100% N 820
4. Do MP students indicate that they have studied content-related areas in their FL?	11. We have learned about science in our FL class.	64% n (524)	18% n (151)	18% n (145)	100% N 820
	12. We have learned about social studies in our FL class.	72% n (596)	14% n (111)	14% n (112)	100% N 819
	13. We have studied about our FL country and used maps	72% n (587)	19% n (156)	9% n (75)	100% N 818
	22. We have made graphs and charts in our FL class.	71% n (582)	15% n (123)	14% n (112)	100% N 817
	10. I can use numbers in my FL.	87% n (720)	9% n (71)	3% n (23)	100% N 814

Source: Saunders (1998).

Table 4.13 also shows the results of the questionnaire responses. The data show that, in response to broad question 1, 90% of Model Program student thought or sometimes thought that learning a foreign language would help them in the future with their job or in school and that three quarters thought their foreign language study would help them with their other subject areas. The students responded favorably to the questions about their foreign language class, with 88-96% responding "yes" or "sometimes" to the questions about liking their foreign language class, enjoying the activities and having fun in class. Most students would like to meet someone from one of their foreign language countries and would like to visit a country where their foreign language is spoken.

Students indicated that they had positive attitudes toward foreign language study and to their foreign language in particular. Most students, 87-93%, were happy to learn their foreign language and wanted to continue to learn their language. They felt special because they could study a foreign language. Responses, although still in the positive domain, were a bit more negative to the questions asking if the students would like to take another foreign language in the future and if their language was difficult to learn. Most students indicated that learning their foreign language was difficult or sometimes difficult; however, they still wanted to continue to study their foreign language. Most students indicated that they were not nervous in class and that they would not be afraid to speak to a person who speaks their language.

In response to the questions about their language skills, students were very confident in their speaking, reading and writing skills. They were less confident in their ability to understand their teacher when he or she spoke in the foreign language. Only 33% indicated that they could understand their teacher and 56% thought that they understood their teacher sometimes. The students' free responses addressed the question of not understanding. Saunders categorized the following responses, "Not being able to understand," "Understanding," "Don't understand," and "Understanding teacher." The issue of understanding was not, however, the most frequently mentioned factor under the "like least" category. The number one response was "Nothing," an indication that students liked everything. Such things as tests, homework, work and getting in trouble were mentioned more frequently than not understanding. Still, it was enough of a concern for students that they listed it in the free responses.

Why would students indicate that they can speak, read and write the language, but only sometimes understand their teacher? Saunders pointed out that this response by the students supports second language acquisition theory (Krashen, 1981, 1987) which stresses the importance of input in the foreign language. Recalling Krashen's input hypothesis, discussed in detail in Chapter 2, the theory says that the teacher should use the foreign language, or provide input, that is just a little above the students' current level. In this way, the teacher prompts the students to move their language ability up to the next level. At this point the teacher again ups the input level by one, and the cycle continues. If the teachers are, indeed, providing language at Krashen's input + 1 level, it would follow that students would perceive that they did not understand everything the teacher was saying. According to this theory, the students are not *supposed* to understand everything. They are to use language learning strategies such as gisting and contextual clues to help construct meaning from unfamiliar language. As seen by the *Model Program Philosophy* (Georgia Department of Education, Curriculum Services, 2002a), the Model Program teachers are committed to conducting 98-100% of the class in the foreign language. The student responses to the questionnaire confirmed that the teachers were fulfilling this commitment. Teachers provided a great deal of contextual support or scaffolding to get their point across. They used pictures, props, puppets, manipulatives, and realia to aid them in getting the concept across without translation. The use of content-related topics, appropriate for the cognitive development of their students and reflecting the expectations delineated in the Georgia statewide curriculum for each grade level, also served to create a familiar context for language learning. So, while students may have believed that they did not understand every word, there was enough contextual support that they were able to develop their language skills. That the students did not indicate a high anxiety level in class is an indication of the good job that the teachers were doing in providing a comfortable, non-threatening atmosphere for language learning. The three reports by the Center of Applied Linguistics (Boyson, 1997; Boyson & Thompson, 1998; Thompson & Boyson, 2001) confirm that the students did, in fact, have good listening comprehension skills. Students might have perceived that they did not understand everything, yet they indicated only moderate anxiety in class, a liking for their foreign language class and the activities they do there, and, by both self-report and by outside evaluation, they did have foreign language listening skills.

Saunders ranked the questionnaire responses from those receiving the most positive responses to those receiving the fewest positive responses and this ranking can be found in Table 4.14. The item receiving the most positive responses was the one indicating students could use numbers in their foreign language. We have seen that the Quality Core Curriculum for K-3 has 14 explicit math-related progress indicators. Such math-related activities as computation, estimation, measurement, telling time, and graphing appear throughout the K-3 curriculum. The self-report of the ability to use numbers provides evidence that Model Program teachers were, in fact, addressing these math indicators in their foreign language classes. Saunders' analysis of ITBS scores showed significant differences in mathematics in favor of students taking a foreign language. The confirmed ability of Model Program students to use numbers in their foreign language provided more direct evidence that if a foreign language program has content-related objectives and the teachers incorporate these objectives into their lessons, it may have a positive effect on content-related areas. As mentioned earlier, there was not a statistical difference in favor of reading, and reading objectives received less emphasis than math objectives. This was confirmed by student responses to the questionnaire. The students' self-report ranked reading 14th out of 25, confirming that they perceived that there was less emphasis on reading than on math.

The top ranked responses indicated that students had studied math (#1) and social studies (#10), including geography (#5), and that students perceived that they could speak (#11) and write (#8) in their for-

Table 4.14. Ranking of Weighted Questionnaire Responses for All Languages

Rank	Question Number	Content
1	10	I can use numbers in (FL)
2	9	I am happy to learn (FL)
3	25	(FL) can help with job/school
4	1	I like (FL) class
5	13	I have studied countries/maps
6	18	I would like to meet a (FL) native speaker
7	5	(FL) class activities are not dull
8	8	I can write some sentences in (FL)
9	16	I want to continue to learn (FL)
10	12	I have learned about community helpers or school in (FL)
11	6	I can speak some sentences in (FL)
12	21	Learning (FL) is important
13	22	I have made charts/graphs in (FL)
14	7	I can read some sentences in (FL)
15	14	I have fun in (FL) class
16	3	I do not feel nervous in (FL) class
17	20	I feel special because I can study (FL)
18	19	I would like to visit a country where they speak (FL)
19	11	I have learned about science in (FL)
20	2	(FL) class is not boring
21	17	I have no interest in studying another foreign language
22	24	I would not be afraid to speak to a person from (FL country)
23	23	(FL) is not difficult to learn
24	4	I understand my teacher when he or she speaks (FL)
25	15	(FL) can help me understand my other subjects

Note: (FL) = French, German, Japanese, or Spanish, depending on language studied.
Source: Saunders (1998, p. 138).

eign language. Students were happy to learn a foreign language (#2), liked their foreign language class (#4) and activities they do there (#7) and wanted to continue to study their foreign language (#9). They thought studying their foreign language would help them in the future (#3) and they would like to meet a native speaker (#6). Students ranked lowest the belief that foreign language study could help them with their other subjects (#25) and their interest in taking another foreign language (#21). They indicated some fear of speaking to a native speaker (#22) and thought learning their foreign language was somewhat difficult (#23). As stated above, they perceived that they could not understand their teacher (#24), a fact refuted by the CAL listening comprehension assessments.

CONCLUSION

Georgia's Elementary School Foreign Languages Model Program has been thoroughly assessed. It succeeds on many levels: positive program assessment, verifiable language proficiency, no interference with and, perhaps, help with basic skills, and positive student attitudes toward learning a foreign language and toward the language classes. The program's initial goal, to offer the successful beginning of an extended sequence to produce proficient speakers of a foreign language, has been achieved. The extensive research performed on the Model Program supports the idea that the content-related and thematically webbed curriculum design is, indeed, appropriate for elementary school foreign language instruction.

NOTE

1. In response to inquiries by auditors from the Georgia Budgetary Responsibility Oversight Committee about what they considered the small comparison sample, Lynn Thompson, CAL researcher, mentioned two factors that influenced the size of the sample. Her response follows.

    - The nature of the assessment. It is important to keep in mind the nature of the assessment that was used. Oral proficiency interviews are administered to two students at a time for 15-20 minutes and involve a trained interviewer and rater. Generally, schools opt to interview a random sample of students from their program. During the interview, students are given a number of performance tasks to elicit a speech sample which is then rated using a rating rubric derived from the ACTFL proficiency guidelines (a nationally recognized standard). We believe that this type of assessment is particularly valid since it mirrors natural language use (and good quality instruction) and this provides us with a genuine view of students' ability to use the target language. Traditional, large-scale assessments, because they consist of multiple-choice items, may be administered to vast numbers of students and therefore result in very large comparison samples. Such assessments cannot, by their very nature, measure oral proficiency skills.

- Assessment of elementary age children in FLES programs is a relatively recent phenomenon and oral proficiency assessment even newer. Georgia is the first and only state that we know of that has assessed the oral proficiency skills of their FLES students using a nationally recognized oral proficiency interview. Our comparison samples are drawn from school districts where we directly oversaw the SOPA administration and evaluation process. (Many other school districts use the SOPA without direct oversight by CAL.) In addition, for the grade level comparisons, we only included students who were of the same grade level and studying a similar language. At the time of the Georgia 2001 evaluation, we did not have samples from 5 times a week programs. (By the way, in the past two years, we have tested students in Grade 5 and Grade 2 in another five times per week program: Georgia results were still higher.)
- We stand by our statement in our report. The Model Program results were compared to all valid SOPA results available at the time. The only clarification I would make is that we compared the Model Program results to results from other elementary school foreign language (FLES) programs only. Model Program results are not higher than known results from partial immersion (half of each school day in the target language) or total immersion (the entire school day in the target language) programs (Thompson, 2003).

CHAPTER 5

CONCLUSION

Our goal has been to describe a FLES program that works and that can serve as a guide for other districts to follow. The 2002-2003 Model Program brochure can be found in Appendix J. Since the Georgia Elementary School Foreign Languages Model Program is a "state-of-the-art model," it is worthy of emulation. It is our sincere wish that our readers will find our information useful and practical.

SUCCESSES

The Georgia Elementary School Foreign Languages Model Program succeeds on many levels and for many reasons. The most important indicator of the program's success is the documented high language proficiency of the students who participate in the program. The fact that the Center for Applied Linguistics found the language assessment results of Georgia Model Program students to be "higher than any known average ELLOPA/SOPA ratings in other foreign language elementary programs in the United States (Thompson & Boyson, 2001, p. 58) confirms that the program is working for its students. Any claims that the program makes as to its effectiveness are supported by research. Not only is student language proficiency documented by CAL, but Saunders' student attitude questionnaire indicates the overwhelmingly positive attitudes toward foreign language study by the student participants. Furthermore, the statistical research validates the content-related curriculum and shows that Model

Program students perform as well as or better than their peers who do not take a foreign language on tests of basic skills.

From the program-level perspective, there are also many strengths. Among them are the staff development component that nurtures new teachers and provides frequent opportunities for collaboration and improvement for all teachers. The Georgia Department of Education invites nationally known experts to work with and train the Model Program teachers, and the instruction they receive reflects the most up-to-date techniques in elementary school foreign language methodology. The maximum eight class teacher workload provides adequate time for teachers to prepare lessons and materials and prevents teacher burnout. Another strength is the workable, articulated curriculum that is tested and revised according to recommendations made by the teachers who implement it and by experts in the field. One of the most important factors leading to student language proficiency is the program requirement that instruction be offered in the target language for 30 minutes daily to all students. The positive results achieved by the Model Program may not be repeated if the model is modified in any way, be it fewer contact hours, less frequency of instruction, less training or a less effective curriculum.

The ongoing, frequent assessments are another strength of this model. Assessments have been performed on all aspects of the program: student language proficiency, student performance in basic skills, student attitudes toward the program, teacher competence, and overall program effectiveness. All of the assessments have had positive results, confirming that the Model Program is achieving its goals. In the era of accountability the Model Program stands up to the test.

What factors have contributed to the success of the Model Program? We believe that one factor is the dedication and expertise of the foreign language specialists and staff at the Georgia Department of Education. In making a serious commitment to the Model Program, they have collaborated with district supervisors and other district level administrators and with teacher trainers at universities in Georgia. Each of these three groups plays an important role in supporting the Model Program. The Department of Education staff administers the program, including the funding and planning of both curriculum development and teacher training. The local system administrators are involved with hiring teachers, overseeing their performance in the classroom, providing them with necessary equipment and materials and releasing them to attend trainings and other special events that highlight the Model Program. The university professors provide courses to better prepare teachers, observe and evaluate teacher performance and assist teachers in completing their certification, when necessary. Furthermore, they all collaborate to enhance and revise the curriculum and to plan the future direction of the Model Program.

Parents, teachers, administrators, community leaders and some government officials have played an important role in supporting the Model Program. While their advocacy may take different forms, they have all made a significant difference. Foreign language teachers maintain active contact with parents and involve them in the program whenever possible. While parents may not always understand the technicalities of how students learn a foreign language or be familiar with the research, they know that they want their children to have the advantage of knowing another language and have lent their time and support to being sure that the Georgia Elementary School Foreign Languages Model Program is refunded each year.

CHALLENGES

We would not be honest if we did not say that there have been and continue to be challenges as this program has grown and developed. We will mention them here with the hope that others can avoid them. Among the challenges are misperceptions about the program, scheduling, shortage of qualified teachers, newcomers enrolling in the program, articulation into middle and high schools and the lack of stable funding. Some decision makers have the false perception that the Model Programs are for "rich white kids." In fact, the most recent demographics as summarized in Table 5.1 show that there are nine out of 19 schools where the majority of the students are nonwhite. Furthermore there are 11 out of 19 schools where more than 40% of students receive free or reduced lunch. This program is designed to serve *all* students within the participating schools, including those with special needs. For example, in 2001-2002, there was one school whose enrollment figures showed 16% of its students were enrolled in ESOL classes, another had 39% of its students in gifted programs and yet another had 25% of its students in special education classes.

Although many administrators like the idea of having an elementary school foreign language program and have a certain amount of good will, they can be overwhelmed with all that must be included in the daily elementary schedule. With the emphasis on basic skills, they feel pressured to eliminate any offering that they consider nonessential. We hope that the research we have presented will convince them that a quality FLES program can provide a rich opportunity for supporting the regular curriculum and does not interfere with student performance on basic skills tests. Some principals try to skirt the Model Program recommendations by scheduling more than eight classes per day for their foreign language teachers or by modifying the schedule to fewer than five days per week.

Table 5.1. 2001-2002 Demographics of Model Program Schools by Percents

School	Race/Ethnicity				Free or Reduced Lunch	Special Education	Gifted	ESOL
	Black	White	Hispanic	Other				
Austin	12	79	2	7	4	10	39	3
Brandon*	9	88	1	2	4	7	27	0
Canton	10	68	20	2	49	16	4	8
Centennial Place	90	2	1	7	79	5	10	1
Clairemont*	36	60	1	3	33	19	17	1
College Hts.*	93	4	0	3	61	25	1	0
Fickett	99	0	0	1	91	4	6	0
Glennwood*	55	41	1	4	46	13	9	4
Graysville	0	98	0	2	30	14	14	0
Lake Park	32	61	2	4	19	9	8	3
Little River	3	84	10	2	18	11	9	3
Oakhurst	98	1	0	1	73	18	1	0
Rivers*	41	29	21	9	47	8	13	16
Rowland	92	0	2	6	84	5	8	1
Sherwood	69	30	1	2	47	14	1	0
South Columbia	13	79	1	7	38	12	1	0
Stevens Creek	6	83	1	10	6	6	6	3
Westchester	22	68	1	9	20	7	17	2
Winnona Park*	31	63	1	4	23	9	20	0

Notes: Percents are approximate; * denotes Model Program funded 100% by the local school district.
Source: Georgia Department of Education (2002c).

By so doing, they jeopardize their Model Program status. We hope that we have presented arguments to convince them that the foreign language teachers need to be an integral part of the regular professional staff, including participation in grade level activities within the school and adequate time to plan and to create materials. The daily delivery is one of the most critical components of this successful program. We have seen significantly lesser results from programs in which the frequency of instruction has been reduced. The research by the Center for Applied Linguistics presented in Chapter 4 provides evidence of this fact.

Although some administrators and community members recognize the need for foreign language proficiency for tomorrow's citizens, they have the narrow view that Spanish should be the only language choice. It is the process of learning a second language early that is important. Students will have more than one opportunity to study additional languages as they progress throughout school. Success in the larger global society depends on ability in a variety of languages, not just one.

The foreign language field has suffered from a lack of qualified teachers for some years. As the baby boomers age and retire, that shortage is becoming more acute. We will not surrender and say that teachers cannot be found. Rather, we must be creative and explore various avenues of recruiting teachers. It is essential that staff at state departments of education and local school districts and schools work closely with colleges of education and that they develop partnerships for recruitment purposes with various organizations including the Visiting International Faculty (VIF), the Embassy of Spain and education offices of various foreign governments in order to fill teacher shortages. Although these teachers are fluent in their language and may be effective teachers in their own countries, we recommend intensive training for them in the realities of American culture, children and school environment. When American teachers lack complete certification in the area of foreign language education, they must have the opportunity to take courses necessary for full certification as quickly as possible. In the meantime, they must be provided with support to be successful in the classroom.

Another challenge encountered at all Model Program schools, but some more than others, is the arrival of new students into the program. With support from the teacher or student peers, newcomers in the early grades can be successful in the program. The serious issues arise when students, with no foreign language background, enroll at the school in fourth or fifth grade. While it is often difficult to schedule, the best solution to this problem is to provide separate language instruction in newcomer classes for these students until they have enough proficiency to integrate into the regular language classes. Alternative possibilities can include providing before or after school help, peer tutoring or providing special teacher-developed materials for these students.

Articulation into middle school and high school is a goal of the Model Program that has been difficult to achieve. There are several factors involved. They include the lack of buy-in by middle school and high school administrators who were not part of the original planning, the blending of Model and non-Model Program students in the middle school, the complex schedule of the middle school day and a lack of articulated materials.

It is a continual frustration for all of those involved with the Model Program that there is a lack of stable funding and that many of us spend inordinate amounts of time and energy trying to convince policy makers of the need to fund the program. As stated earlier, we must continually justify the importance of foreign language learning when in most advanced countries of the world it is compulsory for young students to learn at least one additional language in elementary school, and sometimes two. Although the original plan for the Model Program was to eventually have formula funding, with an annual allotment of funds, as of the time of this printing it is still not a reality. While the annual budget of $2,200,000 seems like a large sum, it is only a small fraction of the Georgia Department of Education budget and represents a cost of about $157 per student per year. Is this not a small price to pay to prepare the citizens of the 21st century to be competitive in the global marketplace and to be as nationally secure as possible?

CONCLUSION

Although there have been difficulties in creating and maintaining the Model Program, the successes have far outweighed the challenges encountered. Monolingual adults who have had the opportunity to visit an elementary school foreign language classroom are often awestruck by the facility with which the students understand and speak the target language. When they see children happily engaged in meaningful activities while using the target language, adults are frequently impressed with the experience because their expectations are often quite different. What may not be immediately evident is that each activity, song or game serves a specific purpose and further supports the students' language development. Implementing a quality elementary school foreign language program requires hard work and dedication. Yet all involved recognize that it is more than worth the effort. Every time we observe the enthusiasm of the Georgia Elementary School Foreign Languages Model Program teachers and students, we are proud of the quality of this excellent model.

REFERENCES

Adger, C. (1995). *Georgia Elementary School Foreign Language Model Program: An evaluation*. Washington, DC: Center for Applied Linguistics.

Alkonis, N.V., & Brophy, M.A. (1961). *A Survey of FLES practices*. New York: Modern Language Association of America.

American Council on the Teaching of Foreign Languages. (1986). *Proficiency guidelines*. New York: ACTFL.

Arnall, G.C. (1992). *Innovations in foreign language education*. Washington, DC: Department of Education. (ERIC Document Reproduction Services No. ED 347 835)

Asher, J. (1986). *Learning another language through actions: the complete teacher's guidebook* (3d ed.). Los Gatos, CA: Sky Oaks Publications.

Ausubel, D. (1968). *Educational psychology: a cognitive view*. New York: Holt, Rinehart & Winston.

Baker, C. (1988). *Key issues in bilingualism and bilingual education*. Philadelphia: Multilingual Matters LTD.

Barr-Harrington, P. (1993). Student self-assessment of foreign language performance. In L. Thompson, *K-8 Foreign language assessment: A bibliography* (p. 8). Washington, DC: Center for Applied Linguistics. (ERIC Document Reproduction Service No. 626 269)

Bialystok, E. (1978). A Theoretical model of second language learning. *Language Learning, 28*: 69-83.

Boujon, C. (1985). *Bon appetit! Monsieur Lapin*. Paris: L'Ecole des loisirs.

Boyson, B. (1997). *Listening and Speaking Assessment of Third Grade Students in the Georgia Elementary School Foreign Languages Model Program*. Washington, DC: Center for Applied Linguistics.

Boyson, B., & Thompson, L. (1998). *Student oral proficiency assessment of fifth grade students in the Georgia Elementary School Foreign Languages Model Program.* Washington, DC: Center for Applied Linguistics.

Branam, J. (1997). *A Study of motivation in African American and Caucasian advanced foreign language students.* Unpublished doctoral dissertation, University of Georgia.

Brown, H.D. (1993). *Principles of language learning and teaching* (3rd ed.). Englewood Cliffs, NJ: Prentice Hall Regents.

Bruck, M., Lambert, W.E., & Tucker, G.R. (1979). Problems in early French immersion programs. In M. Black & E. Isabelle (Eds.), *So you want your child to learn French!* Ottawa, Ontario: Canadian Parents for French. (ERIC Document Reproduction Service No. ED 213 248)

Burstall, C. (1970). *French in the primary school: Attitudes and achievement.* Slough: National Foundation for Educational Research in England and Wales.

Burstall, C. (1977). Primary French in the balance, *Foreign Language Annals, 10*(5), 245-252.

Burstall, C. et al. (1974). *Primary French in the balance.* Slough: National Foundation for Educational Research in England and Wales.

Carle, E. (1987). *The very hungry caterpillar* (2nd ed.). New York: Philomel Books.

Center for Applied Linguistics. (1988). *What do YOU think? Language and culture questionnaire.* Washington, DC: Center for Applied Linguistics.

Chomsky, N. (1965). *Aspects of the theory of syntax.* Cambridge, MA: M.I.T. Press.

Cohen, A.D. (1974). The Culver City Spanish immersion program, the first two years. *Modern Language Journal, 58*(3), 95-103.

Cooper, T. (1987). Foreign language study and SAT-verbal scores. *Modern Language Journal, 71*, 381-387.

Cooper, T., Kalivoda, T., & Morain, G., (Eds.). 1990. *Ready, set, go!* Athens, GA: Agee Publishing.

Cummins, J. (1981). *Bilingualism and minority-language children.* Ontario: Ontario Institute for Studies in Education.

Curtain, H. (1993). *An early start: A resource book for elementary school foreign language.* Washington, DC: ERIC Clearinghouse on Languages and Linguistics.

Curtain, H., & Pesola, C.A. (1994). *Languages and children: Making the match* (2nd ed.). White Plains, NY: Longman.

Dahlberg, C.A.P. (2003). Personal Correspondence.

Draper, J., & Hicks, J.K. (2002). *Foreign language enrollments in public secondary schools, Fall.* New York: American Council on the Teaching of Foreign Languages. [U.S. Department of Education, International Research and Studies Program, Grant # P017A000017-01]

Duncan, G., & Swender, E. (1998). ACTFL performance guidelines for K-12 learners. *Foreign Language Annals, 4*, 479-491.

Eddy, P. (1981). *The Effect of foreign language study in high school on verbal ability as measured by the Scholastic Aptitude Test-Verbal. Final report.* Washington, DC: Center for Applied Linguistics. (ERIC Document Reproduction Service No. ED 196 312)

Egan, K. (1979). *Educational development.* New York: Oxford University Press.

Ellis, R. (1986). *Understanding second language acquisition*. Oxford: Oxford University Press.

Ely, C. (1986). Language learning motivation: A descriptive and causal analysis. *The Modern Language Journal, 70*, 28-35.

Gardner, D.P. (1983). *A Nation at Risk: The imperative for educational reform*. Washington, DC: U.S. Department of Education.

Gardner, R. (1985). *Social psychology and second language learning: The role of attitudes and motivation*. London: Edward Arnold.

Gardner, R., & Lambert, W. (1959). Motivational variables in second-language acquisition. *Canadian Journal of Psychology, 13*, 266-272.

Gardner, R., & Lambert, W. (1972). *Attitudes and motivation in second-language learning*. Rowley, MA, Newbury House.

Gardner, R., & Smythe, P. (1974). Motivation and second-language acquisition. *Canadian Modern Language Journal, 31*. 218-230.

Gardner, R., & Smythe, P. (1981). On the development of the Attitude/Motivation Test Battery. *Canadian Modern Language Review, 37*, 510-525.

Garfinkel, A., & Tabor, K. (1991). Elementary school foreign languages and English reading achievement: A new view of the relationship. *Foreign Language Annals, 24*, 375-382.

Geigle, R. (1957). Foreign language and basic learnings, *Elementary School Journal, 57*, 418-420.

Genesee, F. (1984). Historical and theoretical foundations of immersion education. In J. Lundin & D. P. Dolson (Eds), *Studies on immersion education: A collection for United States educators*. Sacramento, CA: California Department of Education, Office of Bilingual Bicultural Education. (ERIC Document Reproduction Service No. ED 239 509).

Georgia Department of Education. (1996). *Georgia Department of Education 1995-96 report cards*. Atlanta, GA: Author.

Georgia Department of Education. (2002). *Georgia Department of Education 2001-2002 report cards*. Atlanta, GA: Author.

Georgia Department of Education, Curriculum Services (1991). *Elementary School Foreign Languages Model Program Application Form*. Atlanta: Author.

Georgia Department of Education, Curriculum Services (2002a). *Quality Core Curriculum: Ancillaries: Foreign Language Index: Philosophy and Pedagogy*. Atlanta: Author.

Georgia Department of Education, Curriculum Services (2002b). *Quality Core Curriculum: Ancillaries: Foreign Language Index: Modern Languages K-5*. Atlanta: Author.

Gordon, O., Engar, K., & Shupe, D. (1963). *Challenging the superior student by making the study of Russian available in the elementary school curriculum via television*. U.S. Office of Education Grant No. 7-54-0050-024. Salt Lake City: University of Utah.

Hakuta, K. (1984). *The causal relationship between the development of bilingualism, cognitive flexibility and social-cognitive skills in Hispanic elementary school children*. Rosslyn, VA: National Clearinghouse for Bilingual Education.

Hancock, C., Lipton, G., & Baslaw, A. (1976). A study of FLES and non-FLES pupils' attitudes towards the French and their culture. *French Review, 49,* 717-722.

Handcock, M. et al. (1995). *Student perceptions of an elementary foreign language curriculum.* Paper presented at the Annual Meeting of the Eastern Educational Association. Hilton Head, SC. (ERIC Document Reproduction Service No. ED 392 249)

Heining-Boynton, A.L. (1991). The FLES Program Evaluation Inventory (FPEI). *Foreign Language Annals, 24,* 193-202.

Heining-Boynton, A.L. (1992). Reinforcing the elementary school curriculum with content-based FLES. In R. Terry, (Ed.), *Making a world of difference. Dimension: Language '91.* (pp. 57-67). Valdosta, GA: Southern Conference on Language Teaching. (ERIC Document Reproduction Service No. ED 357 646)

Iowa test of basic skills teachers' guide, forms G and H. (1990). Chicago: Riverside Publishing Co.

Johnson, C., Ellison, F., & Flores, J. (1963). The Effect of foreign language instruction on basic learning in elementary schools. *Modern Language Journal, 47,* 8-11.

Krashen, S. (1981). *Second language acquisition and second language learning.* Oxford: Pergamon Press.

Krashen, S. (1987) *Principles and practice in second language acquisition.* Englewood Cliffs, NJ: Prentice-Hall.

Krashen, S., Long, M., & Scarcella. (1979). Age, rate, and eventual attainment in second language acquisition, *TESOL Quarterly, 13,* 373-82.

Krashen, S., Stephen, C., Robin, C., Scarcella, & Long, M. (1982). *Child-adult differences in second language acquisition.* Rowley, MA: Newbury House.

Krashen, S., & Terrell, T. (1983). *The natural approach to language acquisition in the classroom.* Oxford: Pergamon Press; San Fransisco: Alemany Press.

Lambert, W.E., & Tucker, G.R. (1972). *The bilingual education of children: the St. Lambert experiment.* Rowley, MA: Newbury House.

Lambert, W., Tucker, G., & d'Anglejan, A. (1965). Cognitive and attitudinal consequences of bilingual schooling: The St. Lambert Progect through grade five, *Journal of Educational Psychology, 65*(2), 141-59.

Larson-Freeman, D., & Long, M. (1991). *An introduction to second language acquisition research.* New York: Longman.

Lebach, S. (1974). *A report on the Culver City Spanish immersion program in its third year: Its implications for language and subject matter acquisition, language use and attitudes.* Unpublished master's thesis. University of California at Los Angeles, Los Angeles.

Lefrancois, G. (1982). *Psychological theories and human learning.* Monterey, CA: Brooks/Cole Publishing Company.

Leino, B., & Haak, L. (1963). *The teaching of Spanish in the elementary schools and the effects on achievement in other subject areas.* Washington, DC: United States Office of Education.

Levenson, S., & Kendrick, W. (1967). *Readings in foreign languages for the elementary school.* Waltham, MA: Blaisdell Publishing Company.

Liskin-Gasparro, J. (1982). *ETS Oral Proficiency Testing Manual.* Princeton, NJ: Educational Testing Service.

Long, M., & Porter, P. (1985). Group work, interlanguage talk, and second language acquisition. *TESOL Quarterly, 19,* 207-228.

Lopato, E. (1963). FLES and academic achievement. *French Review, 36,* 499-507.

Louisiana State Department of Education, Foreign Languages Section. (1993). *A Guide for administrators: Elementary foreign languages programs in Louisiana Schools.* Bulletin No. 1536. Baton Rouge: Louisiana. State Department of Education. (ERIC Document Reproduction Services No. ED 362 031)

Louton, Z., & Louton, R. (1992). *Flesh out your FLES program: Developmental sequences in teaching units.* (ERIC Document Reproduction Services No. ED 375 636)

McLaughlin, B. (1987). *Theories of second-language learning.* London: Edward Arnold.

McLaughlin, B., Rossman, T., & McCloud, B. (1983). Second language learning: An information processing perspective, *Language Learning, 33,* 135-158.

National Standards in Foreign Language Education Project. (1996). *Standards for foreign language learning: Preparing for the 21st century.* Lawrence, KS: Allen Press.

O'Rourke, E., & the California State Department of Education. (1967). Levels of learning French. In S. Levenson & W. Kendrick (Eds.), *Readings in foreign languages for the elementary school.* Waltham, MA: Blaisdell Publishing Company.

Page, M.M. (1966). We dropped FLES. *Modern Language Journal, 50,* 139-141.

Piaget, J. (1963). *The language and thought of the child.* New York: W.W. Norton.

President's Commission of Foreign Language and International Studies. (1979). *Strength through wisdom: A critique of U.S. capability.* Washington, DC: United States Government Printing Office.

Rafferty, E.A. (1986). *Second language study and basic skills in Louisiana.* Baton Rouge: Louisiana State Department of Education.

Reistra, M., & Johnson, C. (1964). Changes in attitude of elementary school pupils toward foreign-speaking peoples resulting from a study of a foreign language. *Journal of Experimental Education, 33,* 65-72.

Riverside Publishing. (1996a). *Interpretive guide: Georgia statewide norm-referenced testing program: Spring, 1996.* Chicago: Author.

Riverside Publishing. (1996b). *Riverside 96, Catalog.* Chicago: Author.

Rhodes, N., & Thompson, L. (1990). An oral assessment instrument for immersion students: COPE. In A. Padilla, H. Fairchild, & C. Valadez (Eds.), *Foreign language education: Issues and strategies.* Newbury Park, CA: Sage.

Rhodes, N., Tucker, G., & Clark, J. (1981). *Elementary school foreign language instruction in the United States: Innovative approaches for the 1980s.* (Report No. 000-80-02125). Washington, DC: Center for Applied Linguistics. (ERIC Document Reproduction Service No. ED 209 940).

Saunders, C.M. (1998). *The effect of the study of a foreign language in the elementary school on scores on the Iowa Tests of Basic Skills and an analysis of student-participant attitudes and abilities.* Unpublished doctoral dissertation, University of Georgia, Athens.

Schinke-Llano, L. (1985). *Foreign language in the elementary school: state of the art.* Orlando: Harcourt Brace Jovanovich, Inc.

Simon, P. (1980). *The tongue-tied American. Confronting the foreign language crisis.* New York: The Continuum Publishing Corporation.

Skinner, B.F. (1938). *The behavior of organisms: an experimental analysis.* New York: Appleton-Century-Crofts.

Skinner, B.F. (1957). *Verbal Behavior.* New York: Appleton-Century-Crofts.

Stern, H. H. (1963). *Foreign languages in primary education.* Hamburg: UNESCO Institute for Education.

Stevens, J. (1990). *Intermediate statistics, a modern approach.* Hillsdale, NJ: Lawrence Erlbaum Associates, Publishers.

Tabor, K.E. (1987). The Relationship of reading scores to participation in a FLES program, *Dissertation Abstracts International.* (87), DAI 48-10A: 2564. (University Microfilms No. AA18729802).

Tarone, E. (1988). *Variations in Interlanguage.* London: Edward Arnold.

Thompson, L. (2003). Personal correspondence.

Thompson, L., & Boyson, B. (2001). *Georgia Elementary School Foreign Languages (ESFL) Model Program Assessment: Kindergarten, grade 3 and grade 5.* Washington, DC: Center for Applied Linguistics.

Vollmer, J. (1962). *Evaluation of the effect of foreign language study in the elementary school upon achievement in the high school: Final report.* Somerville, NJ: Board of Education.

Wiggins, G., & McTighe, J. (1998). *Understanding by design.* Alexandria, VA: Association for Supervision and Curriculum Development.

APPENDIX A

ORIGINAL APPLICATION FORM

Georgia Department of Education
Elementary School Foreign Languages
Model Program
Application Form

Congressional District _____
School System _____
School Site(s) _____

System Contact Person _____
Title _____
Address _____

Phone _____
Fax _____
Language To Be Offered _____

Name of Superintendent _____

Signature of Superintendent _____

I. Compliance with Program Criteria

If awarded a grant to begin an elementary school foreign language program, does the system agree to the following?

YES	NO	
		Subscribe to a FLES program model for the site(s);
		Follow the foreign language curriculum guides supplied by the Georgia Department of Education;
		Provide foreign language instruction for all kindergarten students in the selected site(s) during Year I and the following grades (through grade 4) in years 2 – 5 (provided the Georgia Legislature continues program funding);
		Provide foreign language instruction for a minimum of 30 minutes daily for each kindergarten student and in grades 1-4 as the program continues;
		Employ a teacher with foreign language certification or a native speaker of the selected foreign language who has K-4 certification and who is willing to complete the K-8 foreign language methods course;
		Pay the salary and benefits difference;
		Ensure that the kindergarten teacher will attend all in-service programs provided by the Georgia Department of Education;
		Commit to support the program for a five year period provided the state legislature continues to fund the program.

II. Local Program Description
    A. How many kindergarten classes are projected at the proposed site(s) for school year 1991- 92?
    B. On an attached sheet, describe a sample daily schedule and work setting for the kindergarten FLES teacher. Include a description of:
        1. Where the foreign language teacher will teach (i.e. in his/her own classroom or floating with a materials cart);
        2. The kind of storage and work area that will provided;
        3. Scheduling of planning time for the foreign language teacher with the kindergarten classroom teachers;
        4. Any other details which are relevant to the success of the program.

C. You may provide letters of support/endorsement for selection of your proposed site(s). Supply no more than five letters.

D. The Department of Education anticipates many more applications for grants than it will be able to award. In such case, the enumeration of additional support for the program from the school system will be a deciding factor in making these awards. In the space below, please provide evidence of additional support which the system will give to the program should it be funded. (Attach additional pages, if necessary.)

E. What is the current transience rate at the proposed site(s)?
_____

F. Since the elementary school foreign language curriculum reinforces a great deal of the regular kindergarten objectives, will the usual kindergarten materials/resources be available to the kindergarten foreign language teacher?

G. Indicate in order of priority the choice of foreign language for your proposed program.

1. _____ 2. _____

3. _____

III. Program Dissemination

A. Is the system willing to serve as a demonstration site to other schools interested in an elementary school foreign language program?

_____ Yes _____ No

If the answer above is yes, how would the system promote being a demonstration site?

B. How will the system integrate the foreign langue program with the total school program?

C. How will the system plan to evaluate the elementary school foreign language program?

D. What efforts would the system make to involve the community in this project?

IV. Articulation

With the initiation of the elementary school foreign language program in your system, what changes would be necessary in the middle/junior high school and high school foreign language programs?

APPENDIX B

THE GEORGIA ELEMENTARY SCHOOL FOREIGN LANGUAGES MODEL PROGRAM ORIGINAL FIFTEEN SITES

Congressional District Number	Name of School System	Name of Schools	Language
First District	McIntosh County	Todd Grant ES	Spanish
Second District	Dougherty County	Lake Park ES Sherwood ES	Spanish
Third District	Pulaski County	Pulaski County ES	Spanish
Fourth District	Dekalb County	Austin ES Rowland ES	German
Fifth District	Atlanta Public	Morris Brandon ES E. Rivers ES	French
Fifth District	Fulton County	Mimosa ES	Japanese
Sixth District	Coweta County	Newnan Crossing ES Western ES	French
Sixth District	Paulding County	McGarity ES	Spanish
Seventh District	Rome Public Schools	West Central ES West End ES	Spanish

(continued)

Congressional District Number	Name of School System	Name of Schools	Language
Seventh District	Walker County	Chattanooga Valley ES Fairyland ES	German
Eighth District	Telfair County	Telfair County Primary	Spanish
Ninth District	Gwinnett County	Rockbridge ES	Spanish
Ninth District	Habersham County	Baldwin ES Demorest ES	Spanish
Ninth District	Lumpkin County	Lumpkin County ES Long Branch ES	French
Tenth District	Elbert County	Blackwell ES Beaverdam ES	Japanese

APPENDIX C

APPROXIMATE BUDGET FOR BEGINNING AN ELEMENTARY FOREIGN LANGUAGE PROGRAM WITH 15 TEACHERS

Topics	Cost per teacher	Total Cost
Teachers (15)		
Salary and Benefits	40,000.00*	600,000.00
Professional Development		
Summer stipend (one week)	400.00	6,000.00
Three trainings during year (6 days & conference)	790.00	11,850.00
Consultants' fees		20,000.00
Curriculum Revision and Enhancement		
Curriculum refinement (10 days × 4 teachers × $100/day)		4,000.00
Materials included with curriculum		1,000.00
Materials and Supplies		
Teacher Materials	1,000.00	15,000.00
General Materials	100.00	1,500.00
Assessment		
of program, of teachers and of students		10,000.00
		669,350.00
Total		

* based on an approximate salary and benefits

APPENDIX D

PHILOSOPHY AND PEDAGOGY

Introduction to Elementary School Foreign Language Curriculum K-5

Philosophy and Pedagogy

The Georgia Elementary School Foreign Languages Model Program advocates a language learning philosophy that includes many tenets. Below are those Statements of Understanding for elementary school foreign language instruction which also apply to middle school as well as high school foreign language teachers. These tenets are listed below.

Foreign language teachers should:

- Teach 98-100% of the time in the target language.
- Use the target language for classroom management as well as for instruction.
- Avoid using translation as a tool for clarifying meaning.
- Help learners to clarify meaning and express understanding without translation.
- Provide learners with a rich target language environment that includes extended listening opportunities such as narration, descriptions, and explanations.

- Provide learners with meaningful concrete experiences, making extensive use of visuals, props, realia, and hands-on activities.
- Present vocabulary in chunks and in context rather than as isolated words or lists.
- Plan and teach around a theme.
- Seek ways to include meaningful culture content in every lesson and every unit.
- Seek to integrate concepts from the general elementary school curriculum in every lesson and every unit.
- Use songs and rhymes to reinforce meaning and practice language.
- Choose authentic songs, games, stories, and rhymes in preference to translations whenever possible.
- Incorporate communicative use of reading and writing from early stages of instruction.
- Plan lessons to include a variety of activities, student groupings, and types of interaction that will appeal to differing learner interests and learning styles.
- Provide opportunities for learners to express personal meaning from the earliest stages of the program.
- Encourage growing independence and independent language use on the part of learners, moving them toward increased expression of individual ideas and opinions.
- Assess learner progress frequently and regularly using a variety of types of assessment.
- Use a variety of strategies to maintain frequent and regular contact with parents.
- Communicate regularly with classroom teachers about student progress and program goals and content.
- Work closely with other teachers in the program to plan curriculum and resolve issues.
- Seek frequent opportunities for professional and language development.
- Maintain open communication about the program and student progress among teachers, administrators, and the general public.

Copyright 1999-2002 Georgia Department of Education. All Rights Reserved.

APPENDIX E

THIRD GRADE WEBTHEME *ALL ABOUT ME*: LANGUAGE STRUCTURES, PROGRESS INDICATORS, VOCABULARY, OBJECTIVES AND ASSESSMENT RECOMMENDATIONS

All About Me
Third Grade
Language Structures Used by Students

It is ____ or/and ____ .	He/She needs ____ .
It is ____ not ____ .	I like to (verb expressing sport oractivity).
I am (verb).	In (activity)
	I use/exercise my ____
He/She is (verb).	I am ___ .
We/They are (verb).	I am going to do ____ .
I like to/don't like to (verb) (objective).	I am good at/strong in (activity/subject).
(subject)	The/A/An (subject) (verb) (object).
always/sometimes/never(verb).	What do you like?
Who is ____?	very
Who does ____?	I want ____ .
Who (verb)?	This/That/It is...
I (verb) and/or (verb).	yes/no

My _____ is _____ .   I/me
My _____ is _____ not _____ .   my/mine
I have _____ (and _____).   you/your
He/She has _____ (and _____).   the/a/an
We/They have _____ (and _____).   He/She needs _____ .
My _____ likes to (verb).
My _____ needs _____ .

Progress Indicators

1. The students will describe, compare, and contrast the responsibilities of different family members at home.
2. Students will identify and summarize various components of pet care.
3. Students will provide autobiographical information in oral and written form.
4. Students will report on activities outside of school.
5. Students will determine which body parts are exercised in certain games and/or sports activities.
6. Students will identify selected foods in the native and target cultures and categorize them according to mealtimes.
7. Students will describe and discuss a balanced meal using the food pyramid.
8. Students will contrast positive and negative character traits in real and fictional characters.
9. Students will use knowledge of character traits to discuss fairytales.
10. Students will compare and contrast fairytales from the U.S. and the target culture.

Thematic Vocabulary Used in Teaching Second Language

Family Members Help Each Other

responsibilities	to clean
to describe	to make the bed
to compare	to iron clothes
to contrast	to set the table

to cook	to cut the grass
meal	to work
to wash dishes	to have to
to wash clothes	to care for

I Can Take Care of a Pet

to feed	cage
to wash/to bathe	dish
veterinarian	tank
shot	to buy
bone	full
leash	empty
collar	to exercise
toys	to need
basket	to want

So Many Things To Do Outside of School

schedule	night
baseball/softball	video games
soccer	always
karate	muscle
dance	heart
gymnastics	bone
swimming	to use
tennis	to be about to/going to do
music	to go to
board games	morning
evening	afternoon

We Are All Unique

characteristics/traits	intelligent
selfish	shy/timid
to lie	quiet (in nature)
liar	lazy
nice	hard-working
friendly	loud
mean/unfriendly	rude
to share	polite
attentive/helpful	outgoing

Fairytales	
fairytale	middle
character	end
magic	beautiful
to transform/to change	ugly
opposites	"once upon a time"
to act out	"and they lived happily ever after"
beginning	to tell

Healthy Eating	
breakfast	vegetable group
lunch	fruit group
dinner	dairy products group
food pyramid	meat, fish and eggs group
sweets	fats, oils and sugars group
breads and cereral group	oils
fats	more of
serving	less of

Third Grade Objectives

Objectives for Students Completing Grade 3 in the Georgia Elementary School Foreign Languages Model Program

ESFL Model Program: Third Grade
These objectives make the following assumptions:

- Student performances are supported by appropriate scaffolding and guidance on the part of the teacher.
- Students have been in the program at least from grades one through three.
- Accommodations must be made for special needs students and for students who have been in the program less than three years.
- Some objectives may appear later for Japanese students.

Note: Numbers in parentheses are references to the *Standards for Foreign Language Learning: Preparing for the 21st Century*. By the end of Grade 3, students will be able to:

3.1 Read for enjoyment using the second language. (1.2, 4.2)

3.2 Read linguistically and developmentally appropriate passages including, but not limited to articles, stories, and other texts. (1.2)

3.3 Read to find needed information. (1.2, 3.2)

3.4 Write using sentences or clusters of language. (1.3)

3.5 Write short texts on topics of personal interest, such as letters and illustrated stories. (1.3, 5.2)

3.6 Summarize personal information or research that they have done, based on templates or models in the target language. (1.3)

3.7 Demonstrate comprehension of extended written and oral discourse. (1.2)

3.8 Begin to self-edit for a variety of purposes. (1.3)

3.9 Retell or paraphrase main elements of a story or passage. (1.2, 1.3)

3.10 Use the target language for a variety of extended spoken activities, such as skits, dialogues, plays, poems, research reports for a variety of audiences. (1.3)

3.11 Share information of their choice with audiences outside the classroom. (1.3, 4.1)

3.12 Ask for information and make requests of teachers and other language speakers. (1.1)

3.13 Provide information and respond to requests from teachers and other language speakers. (1.1)

3.14 Communicate orally and in writing using sentences, as appropriate, with some use of extended discourse. (1.1)

3.15 Follow and begin to give complex instructions. (1.1)

3.16 Demonstrate an understanding of a variety of speech sources (teacher, peers, native speakers, other target language speakers, tapes, CD-Roms, and videos). (1.2, 5.2)

3.17 Recognize the target language when spoken in a variety of dialects and respond with efforts to communicate. (1.2, 4.1)

3.18 Identify geographic areas where the target language is spoken. (3.1)

3.19 Identify examples or influences of the target language and cultures in their own community. (4.1, 4.2)

3.20 Identify, compare, and contrast diverse cultural practices and products, including language, emphasizing similarities as well as differences. (4.1, 4.2)

3.21 Identify selected works of art, music, and literature of the target cultures. (3.1, 3.2)

3.22 Use culturally appropriate language and behavior in both formal and informal target language situations (greeting, leave-taking, eating customs, travel, school, etc.). (1.1, 2.1)

3.23 Use the target language in appropriate content-related areas including, but not limited to, mathematics, social studies, science, literature and fine arts. (3.1)

3.24 Maintain simple conversations in the present tense on a variety of familiar topics. (1.1)

3.25 Participate actively in classroom experiences with music, sports, games, songs, dance, or musical instruments from the target cultures, and extend these experiences into their personal lives. (2.1, 5.2)

3.26 Use information obtained through the target language and cultures to satisfy personal needs and interests. (5.2)3.27 Begin to identify work-related applications of language proficiency. (5.1)3.28. Attempt to create with language at the sentence level. (1.1, 1.3)

3.29 Draw from a basic vocabulary that permits exchanges of a personal nature and on simple academic topics. (1.1, 1.3)

3.30 Demonstrate understanding of natural classroom speech at a normal rate of speed, with limited artificial nonverbal support. (1.1, 1.2)

3.31 Recognize linguistic patterns that occur in the foreign language and compare them with native language patterns. (4.1)

3.32 Use linguistic patterns in limited monitoring of speech and writing. (1.1, 1.3)

NOTE: This does not imply analytical treatment of grammar, or a focus on grammatical drill

Assessment Recommendations

Foreign Language Assessment Recommendations

Quality Core Curriculum Third Grade

The following are only suggested assessment strategies. Teachers are encouraged to develop additional strategies.

FL.3.1 Read books produced by other groups of students, or share them with younger grades.

FL.3.2 Read and discuss target culture cartoons or brief articles from children's magazines working in groups and then share them with whole class.

FL.3.3 Read school schedules and report cards from target countries in pairs to determine type of school subjects, grading system and number of contact hours typical for peers abroad. Compare information gained with other students.

FL.3.4 Create big books by writing brief summaries of familiar stories, fairy tales, or topics of personal interest and illustrating them.

FL.3.5 Share information about pet care as a whole class, as teacher records student contributions. Write and illustrate personalized pet care manuals for a pet of choice.

FL.3.6 Compare information gained from analyzing school schedules and report cards, and write brief summaries of findings.

FL.3.7 Listen to a story or fairy tale on tape and answer comprehension questions.

FL.3.8 Write and revise a rough draft of a composition according to a teacher's checklist.

FL.3.9 Outline a story and retell it to a group.

FL.3.10 Create dialogues for specific scenes from a fairy tale or story and act them out in front of the whole class, another grade or the entire school.

FL.3.11 Create display boards with information on school subjects, schedules and grading in target country schools and exhibit them in the media center.

FL.3.12 Play a game using humorous commands directed towards other students and teacher.

FL.3.13 Follow a series of directions given by the teacher or a fellow student and arrive at a final destination. (Oversized floor maps of a community may be used for this activity.)

FL.3.14 Present orally the main ideas found in a story or short text and create sentence strips to convey important elements.

FL.3.15 Construct an object of cultural significance by following teacher's directions. Instruct students in younger grades to complete similar project.

FL.3.16 View a video segment and fill out a rubric regarding specified information about the characters.

FL.3.17 Hold a basic conversation with an exchange student from a target country.

FL.3.18 Color in countries where the target language is spoken on a map of the world.

FL.3.19 Identify in the yellow pages target language businesses and restaurants.

FL.3.20 Inspect a target culture catalog or brochure and compare to a similar item from the native culture.

FL.3.21 Listen to and identify a current popular song from a target language culture.

FL.3.22 Act out a restaurant scene which incorporates correct table manners.

FL.3.23 Estimate how much a trip to a target language country would cost and convert from dollars to target language currency.

FL.3.24 Draw a conversation card from a box and improvise a short conversation in pairs.

FL.3.25 Present a lip sync to a current popular target culture song.

FL.3.26 Examine travel brochures and select a place to vacation.

FL.3.27 Invite guests who use the target language to "Career Day."

FL.3.28 Write 3-5 sentences about a familiar picture.

FL.3.29 Dictate multiplication problems to one another.

FL.3.30 Identify the object or action that the teacher has described/performed.

FL.3.31 Use column choices to formulate original sentences.

FL.3.32 Peer edit a brief composition.

© Copyright 1999-2002 Georgia Department of Education. All Rights Reserved.

APPENDIX F

JOE FRANK URIZ'S UNIT PLAN

FORL 4025/FORL 6125

Dr. Carol M. Saunders Semonsky
Georgia State University

Elementary School Unit Plan

Name *Joe Frank Uriz*

Language *Spanish*   Grade *Third Grade*

Unit Theme *Mi Animal Domestico*   Web topic *All About Me*

Story form unifier *Yo puedo cuidar a mi animal domestico.*

A. Progress indicators related to theme (omit, for scenarios)

- 3.1 The students will describe, compare, and contrast the responsibilities of different family members at home (who takes care of the pet).

Appendix F

- 3.2 Students will identify and summarize various components of pet care.
- 3.4 Students will report on activities outside of school (taking care of pet).
- 3.5 Students will determine which body parts are exercised in certain games and/or sports activities.
- 3.25 Students will identify, describe and manipulate the currency of a target country (buying a pet).

B. Language functions needed (for scenarios, list your own)

I like to/don't like to (verb).	Me gusta hacer/No, no me gusta hacer
I like to (verb expressing activity).	Me gusta
My _____ is _____.	Mi _____ es _____.
What do you like?	¿Que te gusta?
My _____ is _____ not _____.	Mi _____ es _____ no _____.
Very	Mucho
I have _____ (and _____).	Yo tengo _____ (y _____).
I want _____.	Yo quiero _____.
He/She has _____ (and _____).	El/Ella tiene _____ (y _____).
this/That/It is…	Esta/eso/El es…
We/They have _____ (and _____).	Nosotros/Ellos tienen _____ (y _____).
yes/no	Si/no
My _____ likes to (verb).	Mi _____ le gusta _____.
I/me	Yo/mi
My _____ needs _____.	Mi _____ necesita _____.
my/mine	mi, mio
you/your	tu, tuyo
the/a/an	el/la un/una

C. Vocabulary indicated in curriculum
 (for scenarios, list your own vocabulary)

to feed (dar a comer)	cage (la jaula)
to wash/to bathe (dar un baño)	dish (el plato)
veterinarian (el veterinario)	tank (el tanque)
shot (el pinchazo)	to buy (comprar)
bone (el hueso)	full (lleno)
cage (la jaula)	bed (la cama)
leash (la correa)	empty (vacío)
collar (el collar)	to exercise (hacer ejercicio)

toys (los jugetes)
basket (la cesta, la canasta)
brush (el peine)
fetch (traiga)
jump (salta)

to need (necesitar)
to want (querer)
comb (el cepillo)
sit (siéntese)

Recycled First Grade

pets (las mascotas)
cat (el gato)
rabbit (el conejo)
turtle (la tortuga)

dog (el perro)
bird (el pajaro)
fish (el pez)
snake (la culebra)

What is your favorite pet? (¿Que es tu mascota favorita?)
My favorite pet is... (Mi mascota favorita es...)
My _____'s name is... (Mi _____ se llama_____)

D. & E. Broad Language Objectives and Broad Language Assessments

Broad Language Objective(s)
- Students will describe their pets, and the responsibilities in caring for their pet.
- Students will describe "going to the vet," and doctor procedures.

Broad Language Assessment(s)
- La Mascota de la Semana (Assessment)
- Skit Presentations/Students present their pets (Assessment)
- Skit Presentations/ "Going to the Vet"

F. Create a content-related web (attach). The web is located in Chapter 3, Figure 3.2.

G. & H. Describe your activities (G) and the scaffolding (H) you will use to implement them in the target language.

Activity Idea Introduction/ID Stage	Scaffolding
• Introduction of Sr. Uriz' pet photos	• Sr. Uriz shares his pet photos with the class; describing them and telling their names with sentence strips (scaffold).
• Mystery Basket of Pets	• Students venture to the mystery basket to pull various plush pets. Scaffold on chart paper: Sentences indicating type of animal, color, and the sound the animal makes. Es un/una... Es el color... y hace asi jau, jau o meow, meow.
• Felt Pet Identification/Story	• Students are introduced to ID pets with a felt board and felt pets. Teacher scaffolds with felt pets and story.
• ID Pets/Picture File	• Students practice identifying/naming pets and pet responsibilities (picture file of vet, items used for caring of pet)

134 Appendix F

- Animal Concentration
  - Animal Concentration Students will be presented with the various pets on 8x11 flash cards of pictures of pets (duplicates). Students will practice again on the pets' names (el perro, el gato, el pajáro, el conejo, el pez, la tortuga, la culebra, ¿Qúe es tu animal favorito?, ¿Cómo se llama?)

- Mystery Trunk "Yo puedo cuidar..."
  - Students are presented with a decorated mystery trunk of animals, pet care items and pictures related to the responsibilities in caring for a pet.

- Taking Care of Pet/TPR
  - Sentence strips are used to scaffold. Plush pets are brought out and items of responsibility, e.g. brush, collar, leash, pet toys etc.

- Die Cut Pet Graph
  - Students are asked by the teacher what pet they have at home or to create an imaginary pet, and they are given a die cut to place on the graph in the proper named space on the butcher paper. Scaffold on paper "Perro, Gato, Pez, Hamster, etc. A die cut graph with die cuts represents animals that each student has at home or their imaginary pets.

- Overhead Animal Mania
  - Animal Pie Overhead Transparency game by Scott E. Fredrickson. This is a game that reinforces the vocabulary for different animals, requires students to answer questions about animals and their habitats, and challenges the students' skills in spatial relations. Teacher displays a transparency with a round pie divided into eight sections with animal transparency hidden in the pie. The pie is covered by paper, cut into eight pie pieces. Students pick a section to unveil in order to guess the animal.

Extended Use/Meaningful Stage

- Classroom Pet Activity/ Animal Center
  - Students will have a classroom pet (fish), and keep a weekly log about the classroom pet. Each week, students draw a picture of the animal. They tell how they have cared for the animal throughout the week. Include a description of the animal and the animal's weekly mass if possible. Note any changes that have taken place in the appearance of the animal.

- Guided Questionnaires/ Interviews on Pets
  - Students interview classmates or friends using a questionnaire format about their family pet.

- Journals on their and friend's pet
  - Students work in pairs designing a list chart of characteristics on their and friend's pet such as name, type of pet, color, activities they do with their pet, and responsibilities. Then using a scaffold (guided writing), they will journal about their pet and a friend's pet.

- Kidpix Software/ Computer Lab
  - Students use Kidpix to design a slide show of taking care of their pet, writing sentences with teacher's guidance for each slide. "Esto es mi perro." "Yo doy agua a mi perro."

- Writing e-mails to friends, faculty and administration
  - Students collaborate and work in pairs writing a guided letter about their pets.

• Smush Book/ *Mi Mascota*	• *Mi Mascota* Students make a smush book. 1. Describe the pet (color, size, characteristics). 2. Tell its name. 3. Tell the sound it makes. 4. Tell what the student does to take care of the pet and finally its name.
• La Mascota de la Semana/Internet	• Students visit the web site: *http://www.yupimsn.com/yupinitos/ mascotas*, and explore the pet of the week (writing in journal information on the pet of the week). Students then explore site to get information on their pets.
• Pet Training	• Children work in small groups to find information about animal training. They are given a guide/list of animals and commands that go along with each pet category. Students match commands/tricks with pictures.
• Pet Inventions	• Children are given an example of a real pet invention such as the "doggie door," a small door in the bottom of a larger door that allows a pet to go outside and come back in freely. Divide children into groups of three. Each group will be asked to come up with one invention with the help of a list of ideas and sentence strips to scaffold. One child in the group writes a paragraph describing the invention with scaffold, another child draws a picture to go with the description, and the third child presents the group's invention to the rest of the class.
Students choose assessment	
• La Mascota de la Semana (Written Assessment)	• Using guide and journals, students imagine their pet is the pet of the week and write a Pet of the Week Profile. "Oye, oye! Leye todo sobre la mascota de la semana…." Students write a description about their pet or imaginary pet to be featured in "La Mascota." Students should write at least five sentences that mention pet name, color, age, descriptors, and how he/she takes care of the pet. Present to class.
• Skit Presentations/ Students present their pets (Oral Assessment)	• Pair Skit where students present a skit based upon their pets. Two friends discuss their pets, and how important it is to take care of their pets (scenarios: going to the doctor, park, pet store, etc.) Videoed

I. Materials, Games, Songs and Total Physical Response Activities

Materials

- Personal Pet Photos
- Picture file of pets/care duties
- Mystery basket

136   Appendix F

- Mystery trunk decorated with "Yo puedo cuidar..." on the outside
- Plush animals for mystery basket and trunk
- Pet supplies for mystery trunk
- Guided questionnaire
- "Hueso" for The Bone Game
- Die cuts of animals for overhead transparency game
- Pie pieces to cover animals in overhead game
- Sentences strips
- Die cuts of pets for graph
- Journals
- Blindfold for game la gata ciega
- Students' photo of pets or a drawn picture of pet
- 3rd grade tablet paper for "Extra, Extra!"
- Construction paper for Extra, Extra!
- Color paper for smush book
- Crayons and pencils for smush book
- Books *Harry el Perrito Sucio por Gene Zion* and *Hally Tosis por Dav Pilkey*
- Computer Lab
- Internet Sites to navigate on "Mascota": *www.perrosygatos.com.ar/ http://www.yupimsn.com/ yupinitos/mascotas*

Games

- *Perro! Perro! Despierta!*

    The dog stands up, removes the blindfold, and goes around the circle, asking: Quien tiene mi hueso? Turning to a player, he then asks: "Angelita, tienes tu mi hueso?" Player 2: "No, no tengo tu hueso." The perro is allowed to ask three players the question. If the student (perro) fails to find the bone on the third try, he/she must return to the center. If he or she finds the hueso, the one who hid it must take his place as perro.

- *Los Animales Grandes, Los Animales Pequenos*

    Two teams may play the game. Pictures of small pets and some of large pets. Teams are selected. The leader asks questions similar to those below of individual students on each team, in turn. Each correct answer scores a point for the team. If a player on one team fails to answer correctly, the other team gets a chance at the question.
    " Cuantos animales grandes hay?"
    "Cuantos animales pequenos hay?"
    "Como se llaman los animales grandes?"
    "Como se llaman los animales pequenos?"
    "Cual de los animales es el mas grande de todos?"

- *Subiendo Las Escaleras*

    A good blackboard game for about 20 players in two teams. The players are divided into two teams and each member has a turn writing a word and "climbing" his team's ladder as quickly as possible. The whole group decides on the kind of words to be written in this case pets, pet homes, pet food, etc. The team filling the spaces on the ladder correctly in the shortest time is the winner. When both ladders have been filled in, the group may take turns using the words in sentences. Then another category of words may be chosen for another round.

- *El Hueso*

    Up to 20 children may play. A cardboard cut-out object resembling a bone may be made, if desired, or an object such as an eraser may be used. A chair is needed for each player, and a blindfold. One player is chosen to be el perro (the dog). He sits blindfolded, supposedly sleeping. All the other players sit in circle around the perro's chair. At a signal from the Leader, a player in the circle stealthily attempts to get the hueso, which has been placed under the perro's chair. If the perro hears the player, he stands up, and the player caught in the act must become the perro. If the child gets the hueso without awakening the perro, he hides it somewhere on his person, perhaps by sitting on it. When a player has done this, all those in the circle say:

    "Perro! Perro! Despierta!" The player says, "No, no tengo tu hueso."

    The perro is allowed to ask three players a question. If he fails to find the bone on the third try, he must return to the center. If he finds the hueso, the one who hid if must take his place as perro.

- *La Gata Ciega*

    In this game the animal and pet supply/necessity changes as the students wish. (outside) Scaffolds used are sentence strips with pets and pet supplies (food, plate, leash, collar, etc.)

    > Gata ciega, ¿qué anda haciendo?
    > Ando buscando una copa de leche
    > ¿Para quien? Para mis gatitos.
    > ¿Y me dará uno?
    > No? Pues, piérdete.

    Then the blind animal chases the other players; the one caught is next pet.

- *Pet Charades*
- *Overhead Guessing Game*

    Using overhead projector and small plastic animals or stencils, the students can try to guess the name of the animal by looking at the shadow.

- *Animal Concentration* using flash cards

138   Appendix F

- *Animal Pie Overhead Transparency Game* by Scott E. Fredrickson

  This is a game that reinforces the vocabulary for different animals, requires students to answer questions about animals and their habitats, and challenges the students' skills in spatial relations. The teacher displays a transparency with a round pie divided into eight sections with animal transparency hidden in the pie, which is covered by paper, cut into eight pie pieces. Students pick a section to unveil in order to guess the animal.

Songs and Total Physical Response (TPR) Activities

- The *Gatito, Perrito* song is a TPR song.
- *Taking care of the animal TPR game* (stuffed animals: gato, perro, pajaro, etc.) students demonstrate pet care with movements such as dar a comer, banar, peinar etc.
- *TPR of playing with your pet* (correr, brincar, andar, buscar, tirar etc.)
- *Mi Gallo* – hand movement song about a pet rooster (traditional Latin American song)

Mi Gallo
Mi gallo bailo ayer
Ya cantara y bailara
Con cocori, cocora
Ya cantara conmigo
Cocori, cocora,
Cocori, cori, cocori, cora
Cocori, cori, cocori, cora

El Sr. Don Gato
Estando el Señor de un gato sentadito en su tejado marrama mia miau, miau, sentadito en su tejado.

El Burrito Va a Atlanta
Arre, mi burrito
Que vamos a Atlanta
Que mañana es fiesta
Y el otro tambien
Arre, arre, arre
Leveme usted al trote
Arre, arre, arre
Lleveme al galope
De prisa, de prisa

El Gatito y El Perrito
(sung to: *La Cucaracha*)
El gatito, el gatito
Corre detras del ratoncito. (run in place)
El gatito, el gatito
Corre, corre y brinca.
El perrito, el perrito
Mira al gatito (look to left, look to right)
El perrito, el perrito
Simplemente quiere dormir. (fall on floor and pretend to sleep).

Mi Mascota
(sung to: *Pop goes the Weasel*)
Mi perro se llama Fido
Mi gato se llama Fuzzy
Mi conejo se llama Hopper.
Yo me llamo ____.
raton, culebra, pez, tortuga, caballo,

Animales en Mi Casa
El perro, el perro
Vive en mi casa, vive en mi casa
Hace asi, hace asi
"____," "____"
(el gato, el pez, la tortuga, y el pajaro)

Era Un Gato Grande
Era un gato grande que hacia ron, ron,
muy acurrucado en su almohadón,
abría los ojos, se hacia el dormido,
movía la cola, con aire aburrido.

Era un ratoncito, chiquito, chiquito,
que asomaba el morro por un agujerito,
desaparecía y volvía a asomarse,

Cinco Pollitos
(Hold hand open, then close your thumb, then your pointer, and then close the other three fingers all at once.)
Cinco pollitos tiene mi tia.
Uno le canta,
Otro le pia,
Y tres le tocan la sinfonia

Gatito or Perrito Jump Rope Rhyme
Gatitio, gatito, puedes saltar
Sí, sí ayúdame, ayúdame a cantar.
Uno, dos, tres, cuatro...

El Perro de Mi Tia
El perro de mi tía tiene una tremenda tos.
El perro de mi tía tiene una tremenda tos.
El perro de mi tía tiene una tremenda tos.
Y lo curan con aceite alcanforaó -guao guao-

Repeat the song. Drop one phrase each time and replace it with a clap until you are clapping the entire song while singing "la la la."

El perro de mi tía tiene una tremenda
(1 clap)
El perro de mi tía tiene una(2 claps)
El perro de mi tía tiene (3 claps)
El perro de mi tía (4 claps)
El perro de (5 claps)
El perro (6 claps)
la la la (all claps) y lo curan con aceite alcanforaó-guao guao-

Miau, miau
Miau Miau, maúlla mi gato, miau, miau,
muy enfadado, porque quiere
que le compre,
un lacito colorado, y yo no se lo
he comprado.
Miau, miau, maúlla mi gato miau, miau,
muy enfadado, por que quiere
que le compre,
un lacito colorado, por qué me
gusta enfadado,
miau, miau, maúlla mi gato.

y hacia un ruido, cri, cri, cri,
con mucho donaire.

Salió el ratoncito, corrió por la alfombra,
que miedo le daba ¡hasta de su sombra!
al dar la media vuelta,
sintió un gran estruendo,
y vio los ojos grandes de un gato tremendo,
sintió un gran zarpazo sobre su lomito
y salió corriendo todo asustadito.

Y aquí acaba la historia de aquel ratoncito
que asomaba el morro por un agujerito

Cinco Ratoncitos /TPR Movement
Cinco ratoncitos de colita gris,
mueven las orejas, mueven la nariz,
abren los ojitos, comen sin cesar,
por si viene el gato, que los comerá,
comen un quesito, y a su casa van,
cerrando la puerta, a dormir se van.

Cu Cú cantaba la rana
Cu cú, cu cú
Cu cú, cu cú
Cu cú cantaba la rana
Cu cú debajo del agua.
Cu cú pasó un caballero
Cu cú con capa y sombrero.
Cu cú pasó una señora
Cu cú con traje de cola.
Cu cú pasó un marinero
Cu cú vendiendo romero.
Cu cú le pidió un ramito.
Cu cú no le quiso dar.
Cu cú y se echó a llorar.

J. QCC Objectives incorporated (numbers and words)

Objectives:

- 3.1 Read for enjoyment using the second language. (1.2, 4.2)
- 3.2 Read linguistically and developmentally appropriate passages including, but not limited to articles, stories, and other texts. (1.2)
- 3.3 Read to find needed information. (1.2, 3.2)
- 3.4 Write using sentences or clusters of language. (1.3)
- 3.5 Write short texts on topics of personal interest, such as letters and illustrated stories. (1.3, 5.2)
- 3.6 Summarize personal information or research that they have done, based on templates or models in the target language. (1.3)
- 3.7 Demonstrate comprehension of extended written and oral discourse. (1.2)
- 3.8 Begin to self-edit for a variety of purposes. (1.3)
- 3.9 Retell or paraphrase main elements of a story or passage. (1.2, 1.3)
- 3.10 Use the target language for a variety of extended spoken activities, such as skits, dialogues, plays, poems, research reports for a variety of audiences. (1.3)
- 3.11 Share information of their choice with audiences outside the classroom. (1.3, 4.1)
- 3.12 Ask for information and make requests of teachers and other language speakers. (1.1)
- 3.13 Provide information and respond to requests from teachers and other language speakers. (1.1)
- 3.14 Communicate orally and in writing using sentences, as appropriate, with some use of extended discourse. (1.1)
- 3.20 Identify, compare, and contrast diverse cultural practices and products, including language, emphasizing similarities as well as differences. (4.1, 4.2)
- 3.24 Maintain simple conversations in the present tense on a variety of familiar topics. (1.1)
- 3.25 Participate actively in classroom experiences with music, sports, games, songs, dance, or musical instruments from the target cultures, and extend these experiences into their personal lives. (2.1, 5.2)
- 3.28. Attempt to create with language at the sentence level. (1.1, 1.3)

- 3.29 Draw from a basic vocabulary that permits exchanges of a personal nature...
- 3.31 Recognize linguistic patterns that occur in the foreign language and compare them with native language patterns. (4.1)
- 3.32 Use linguistic patterns in limited monitoring of speech and writing. (1.1, 1.3)

K. National Standards addressed (numbers and short descriptors)

- 1.1 Interpersonal Communication (Pair guided interviews, Skit Presentations/Students present their pets (Assessment)
- 1.2 Intrepretive Communication (Students demonstrate listening comprehension-Total Physical Response Activities, La Mascota de la Semana (Assessment)
- 1.3 Presentational Communication (Skit Presentations/Students present their pets (Assessment), Kidpix Slideshow, "Mi Mascota" Smush Book (present to peers), Presentation of weekly log of classroom pet, Journals on internet site/pet of the week, Pet Training Manual, Pet Inventions Presentations
- 2.1 Practices and Perspectives of C2 (pets having more freedom in the target culture, roles of pets in target culture)
- 2.2 Products and Perspectives of C2 (pet food in America vs. Europe, South America, Central America, or the Caribbean, authentic pet songs, games (*La Gata Ciega, Perro! Perro! Despierta!, La Llamada de los Animales*)
- 3.1 Reinforce Content Knowledge (Die Cut Pet Graph-mathematics, Overhead Animal Mania/questions on animal's habitat-science, Classroom Pet Activity/Animal Center-science, math, language arts)
- 4.2 Cultural Comparasions (Different types of pets in target vs. American Pets)
- 5.1 Use L2 within and beyond school setting (identify professions where second language is useful (bilingual veterinarian)
- 5.2 Use L2 for enjoyment and enrichment ("Smush Books," skit presentations)

APPENDIX G

JOE FRANK URIZ'S
ASSESSMENT ASSIGNMENTS AND GRADING RUBRICS

Nombre_____ Fecha_____

Mi Mascota

Yo tengo _____. Se llama _____ y tiene
        (mascota)   (nombre)

_____ _____. Es _____ y _____. Su
(edad) (meses o años) (color)   (color)

tamaño es _____.
(pequeño, mediano, grande)

las mascotas
un perro, un gato, un pájaro, un conejo, un pez, una tortuga, una culebra

el nombre
Lassie, Laddie, Benji, Scooby, Flipper, Flex, Garfield

la edad
uno, dos, tres, cuatro, cinco, seis, siete, ocho,
nueve, diez, once, doce, trece, catorce, quince,
diez y seis, diez y siete, diez y ocho, diez y nueve, veinte

los colores
blanco, dorado, negro, café, grís

el tamaño
pequeño, mediano, grande

Parte II

Nombre_____ Fecha_____

Es _____ y _____.
(palabras que describe tu mascota)

Voy al _____ con mi _____. Le gusta
    (lugar)   (mascota)

mucho _____ conmigo.
    (verbo)

las palabras que describe
mimoso, mimosa, juguetón, juguetona, viejo, vieja, joven

los lugares
parque, show de mascotas, vetrinario, tienda de mascotas, Sagamore Hills

los verbos
brincar, correr, jugar

Mis responsabilidades son _____, _____, y
            (responsabilidades)

_____. Necesita _____ y _____
        (objetos para mi mascota)

las responsabilidades
dar comida, dar agua, bañar, limpiar su casa

Los objetos para mi mascota
una pelota, una comida, un collar, una correa,
un peine, un cepillo, una pecera

Joe Frank Uriz's Assessment Assignments and Grading Rubrics

Sagamore Hills Elementary
Spanish

Mi Mascota de la Semana

Name: _____ Teacher: <u>Sr. Uriz</u>
Date: _____ Title of Work: _____

	Criteria				Points
	5 points	**10 points**	**15 points**	**20 points**	
Identifying Type of Pet, Name, and Age	Does not identify type of pet, name, or age.	Identifies type of pet, but does not give a name or age.	Identifies type of pet and name but leaves out age.	Identifies type of pet, name, and age.	____
Describing pet	Student uses incorrect descriptions to describe pet. "Mi perro es azul."	Student uses adjectives but is limited to only color or personality.	Student uses 1 adjective for color and 1 for personality of pet.	Student uses one to two adjectives to describe pet's color and two for personality.	____
Places to take pet	Student does not identify a place to take their pet.	Names one place. Incorrect for their type of pet.	Names one place, but does not identify pet.	Names one place. Identifies pet in the sentence.	____
Pet Care Supplies	Student does not name an item needed for their pet.	Student names an item but does not make sense for their type of pet.	Student names one item used in pet care. (used correctly)	Student names two items used in pet care.	____
Taking care of pet	Student does not identify any responsibilities in pet care.	Names one responsibility.	Names two responsibilities.	Names three responsibilities.	____
				Total---->	100

Teacher Comments:

90–100 = Excellent (E)   70–79 = Needs Improvement
80–89 = Satisfactory (S)   69 and below = Unsatisfactory

Joe Frank Uriz's Assessment Assignments and Grading Rubrics

Expañol con Señor Uriz
Presenting a Mini-Play about My Pet

It's time to have fun and be creative with our "Mi Mascota" unit. You and a friend will need to choose one of the following situations:

- A play presentation where you and your friend take a pet to the veterinarian
- A skit of you and your friend talking about your pets and the responsibilities you have in taking care of them

How do I do my mini-play?

- A fill in the blank sentence strip script in Spanish will help you in your mini-play
- You and a friend will use studded animals and create props to present your play

What do I need to present in my mini-play?

- You will identify your pet's name, age, and features (color of fur and eyes, size)
- Tell your friend how you care for your pet and what supplies are needed
- Please remember to use all the new and exciting words learned in class on taking care of your pet

What do I need for my play?

- You and your friend will bring in stuffed animals, pet supplies and props for your presentation

How much time do I have to present?

- Mini-plays will be videotaped and will be at least 3 to 4 minutes in length

Grading Rubric Attached

Joe Frank Uriz's Assessment Assignments and Grading Rubrics
Sagamore Hills Elementary
Spanish

Skit Presentation on Pets

Name: _____   Teacher: <u>Sr. Uriz</u>
Date: _____   Title of Work: _____

	Criteria				Points
	1	2	3	4	
Creativity in Presentation	Student did not create with the target language, and did not use stuffed animals or pet care props.	Student creates a little with the target language, and uses some stuffed animals, and pet care props.	Student creates and uses stuffed animals, and pet care props.	Student creates with the language and uses an abundance of stuffed animals and pet care props.	28 (score × 7)
Identifies pet	Does not identify	Tells only name	Tells name and age	Tells name, age, and describes pet's features.	20 (Score × 5)
Identify variety of components of pet care	Does not identify components of pet care.	Identifies one pet care component.	Identifies two pet care components.	Identifies three pet care components.	20 (Score × 5)
Pronunciation	Frequently mispronounces words	Hesitation in pronunciation	Correct pronunciation	Correct and flowing	12 (Score × 3)
Language Functions and Vocabulary	Student does not use any vocabulary from Pet Unit.(0 words)	Student uses some of the vocabulary from the Pet Unit. (1 to 2 words)	Student uses a good amount of vocabulary from the Pet Unit. (3 to 4 words)	Student uses an abundance of vocabulary words from the Pet Unit. (5 or more words)	20 (Score × 5)
				Total---->	100

Teacher Comments:

90-100 = Excellent (E) 70-79 = Needs Improvement (N)
80-89 = Satisfactory (S) 69 and below = Unsatisfactory (U)

APPENDIX H

STUDENT ORAL PROFICIENCY ASSESSMENT (SOPA) RATING SCALE

(see next page)

Rating Scale for CAL Oral Proficiency Exam (COPE) and Student Oral Proficiency Assessment
Revised 2000

	Jr. Novice-Low	Jr. Novice-Mid	Jr. Novice-High	Jr. Intermediate-Low	Jr. Intermediate-Mid	Jr. Intermediate-High	Jr. Advanced-Low	Jr. Advanced-Mid	Jr. Advanced-High
Fluency	Produces only isolated words and/or high-frequency expressions such as *good morning* and *thank you*. Has essentially no functional communicative ability.	Uses a limited number of isolated words, two-to three-word phrases, and/or longer memorized expressions within predictable topic areas. May attempt to create sentences, but is not successful. Long pauses are common.	Uses high frequency expressions and other memorized expressions with reasonable ease. Signs of originality are beginning to emerge. Creates some sentences successfully, but is unable to sustain sentence-level speech.	Goes beyond memorized expressions to maintain simple conversations at the sentence level by creating with the language, although in a restrictive and reactive manner. Handles a limited number of everyday social and academic interactions.	Maintains simple sentence-level conversations. May initiate talk spontaneously without relying on questions or prompts. Gives simple descriptions successfully. May attempt longer, more complex sentences. Few, if any, connectors are used.	Maintains conversation with increasing fluency. Uses language creatively to initiate and sustain talk. Emerging evidence of paragraph-like speech with some connected sentences in descriptions and simple narratives, but cannot sustain paragraph-level speech.	Reports facts easily. Can discuss topics of personal interest and some academic topics to satisfy the requirements of school and every day situations. Narrates and describes at the paragraph level, though haltingly at times. False starts are common.	Handles with ease and confidence topics of personal and general interest and some academic topics. Narrates and describes successfully. Connects sentences smoothly, and organizes speech into paragraphs using connectors such as *first, next, finally*, etc.	Handles most social and academic requirements confidently, but may break down under the demands of complex, formal tasks. Organizes and extends speech beyond paragraph. Emerging ability to support opinions and hypothesize on abstract topics is evident.

Grammar

May use memorized, high frequency phrases accurately. Lacks an awareness of grammar and syntax.	Memorized expressions with verbs and other short phrases may be accurate, but inaccuracies are not uncommon. Does not successfully create at the sentence level with conjugated verbs.	Creates some sentences with conjugated verbs, but in other attempts to create sentences, verbs may be lacking or unconjugated. Other grammatical inaccuracies are present.	Verbs are conjugated in present tense, but may be inaccurate. Many other grammatical inaccuracies are common.	Uses mostly present tense verbs although awareness of other tenses (i.e. future or past) may be evident. Many grammatical inaccuracies may be present.	Uses present tense well, but lacks control of the past tenses. May use future tense. Many grammatical inaccuracies may be present. Some awareness of these inaccuracies may be evident.	Uses present, past and future tenses. May effectively self-correct when aware of grammatical inaccuracies. Structures of native language may be evident (e.g. literal translation).	Has good control of present, past and future tenses. Some inaccuracies may remain, but speech is readily understood by native speakers of the language. In some cases, may use nonstandard varieties of grammar.	Uses all verb tenses accurately and sometimes uses increasingly complex grammatical structures. Some patterns of error may persist, but they do not interfere with communication.

	Jr. Novice-Low	Jr. Novice-Mid	Jr. Novice-High	Jr. Intermediate-Low	Jr. Intermediate-Mid	Jr. Intermediate-High	Jr. Advanced-Low	Jr. Advanced-Mid	Jr. Advanced-High
Vocabulary	Uses words in very specific topic areas in predictable contexts. May use a few memorized, high-frequency expressions.	Uses specific words in a limited number of topic areas, high-frequency expressions, and other memorized expressions. Frequent searches for words are common. May use native language or gestures when attempting to create with language.	Uses vocabulary centering on basic objects, places, and common kinship terms, adequate for minimally elaborating utterances in predictable topic areas. Use of native language is common.	Has basic vocabulary for making statements and asking questions to satisfy basic social and academic needs, but not for explaining or elaborating on them. Use of native language is common.	Has basic vocabulary, permitting discussions of a personal nature and limited academic topics. Serious gaps exist for discussing topics of general interest. If speaker lacks precise word, use of circumlocution may be ineffective. May resort to native language.	Has a broad enough vocabulary for discussing simple social and academic topics in generalities, but lacks detail. Sometimes achieves successful circumlocution when precise word is lacking. May use native language occasionally.	Vocabulary is primarily generic but is adequate for discussing concrete or factual topics of a personal nature, topics of general interest, and academic subjects. May use circumlocution successfully when specific terms are lacking.	Has adequate vocabulary for including detail when talking about concrete or factual topics of a personal nature, topics of general interest, and academic subjects. Uses circumlocution effectively. Rarely uses native language.	Uses precise vocabulary for discussing a wide variety of topics related to everyday social and academic situations. Lack of vocabulary rarely interrupts the flow of speech.

Comprehension

| Recognizes isolated words and high frequency expressions. | Understands predictable questions, statements, and commands in familiar topic areas (with strong contextual support), though at a slower than normal rate of speech and/or with repetitions. | Understands simple questions, statements, and commands in familiar topic areas, and some new sentences with strong contextual support. May require repetition, slower speech, or rephrasing. | Understands familiar and new sentence-level questions and commands in a limited number of content areas with strong contextual support. Follows conversation at a fairly normal rate. | Understands sentence-level speech in new contexts at a normal rate of speech, although slow-downs may be necessary for unfamiliar topics. Carries out commands without prompting. | Understands longer stretches of connected speech on a number of topics at a normal rate of speech. Seldom has comprehension problems on everyday topics. (Can request clarification verbally) | (The Advanced-Low category is new with the 1999 revision of the ACTFL Proficiency Guidelines. Revisions to the listening comprehension section of the guidelines are not yet available.) | Understands main ideas and most details in connected speech on a variety of topics, and is aware of connectors, but may be unable to follow complicated speech. May have difficulty with highly idiomatic speech. | Understands complex academic discourse and highly idiomatic speech in conversation. Confusion may occur due to sociocultural nuances or unfamiliar topics. |

Scale based on the *American Council on the Teaching of Foreign Languages (ACTFL) Proficiency Guidelines*, Revised 1999.

APPENDIX I

STUDENT ATTITUDE AND ABILITY QUESTIONAIRE

Student Initials ____
Date of Birth ____

ESFL Model Program Student Questionaire
Spanish

My school: _____
I have studied Spanish for _____ years.
I have visited a country where Spanish is spoken.   YES   NO
Someone in my home usually speakes Spanish.   YES   NO

Please read along with your teacher as he or she reads the following statements. When you answer the questions, think about all the Spanish classes you have had at you school, not just the class you are in today. Use the scale below and circle the face that you think best describes your opinion.

☺ YES   😐 SOMETIMES   ☹ NO

1. I like Spanish class.   ☺ 😐 ☹
2. My Spanish class is boring.   ☺ 😐 ☹
3. I feel nervous in Spanish class.   ☺ 😐 ☹

4. I understand my teacher when she speaks Spanish. ☺ 😐 ☹
5. The activities in my Spanish class are dull. ☺ 😐 ☹
6. I can speak some sentences in Spanish about things we have studied in class, such as my family or school. ☺ 😐 ☹
7. I can read some sentences about what we have studied in class. ☺ 😐 ☹
8. I can write some words or sentences in Spanish. ☺ 😐 ☹
9. I am happy that I can learn Spanish. ☺ 😐 ☹
10. I can use numbers in Spanish. ☺ 😐 ☹
11. We have learned about science, such as animals, plants and planets, in Spanish class. ☺ 😐 ☹
12. We have learned about social studies, such as holidays, transportation and our community workers. ☺ 😐 ☹
13. We study about other countries or read maps. ☺ 😐 ☹
14. I have fun in Spanish class. ☺ 😐 ☹
15. My Spanish class can help me understand my other subjects. ☺ 😐 ☹
16. I want to continue to learn Spanish. ☺ 😐 ☹
17. I have no interest in taking another foreign language one day. ☺ 😐 ☹
18. I would like to meet someone from Mexico or another Spanish-speaking country. ☺ 😐 ☹
19. I would like to visit a country where they speak Spanish. ☺ 😐 ☹
20. I feel special because I can take Spanish. ☺ 😐 ☹
21. Learning Spanish is important. ☺ 😐 ☹
22. We have made charts and graphs in Spanish class. ☺ 😐 ☹
23. Spanish is difficult for me to learn. ☺ 😐 ☹
24. If I met someone from Spain, I would be afraid to speak Spanish to him. ☺ 😐 ☹
25. I think that learning Spanish can help me in the future in my job or at school. ☺ 😐 ☹

Please name some of the things you like best about your Spanish class:

Please name some of the things you like least about your Spanish class:

Source: Saunders (1998)

APPENDIX J

GEORGIA ELEMENTARY SCHOOL
FOREIGN LANGUAGES MODEL PROGRAM BROCHURE,
2002–2003

Georgia Elementary School
Foreign Languages (ESFL)
Model Program

Background

After years of research on the best format for teaching children a second language, the Georgia Elementary School Foreign Languages Model Program was founded in 1992. Funded by a special initiative of the Georgia General Assembly, the program was begun in 10 congressional districts in 15 different school districts. The program began with kindergarten and expanded to add an additional grade level each year, until all children at each site received foreign language instruction *five days a week, thirty minutes each day from Kindergarten through fifth grade*.

Philosophy and Pedagogy

Teachers in the model program adhere to certain guidelines when planning and conducting their lessons. This ensures that all children in the program receive exemplary foreign language instruction that teaches them to communicate in the second language. These guidelines include:

- using the second language 98-100% of the time
- teaching around a theme
- helping students understand without translating
- providing a language-rich environment that presents vocabulary in context
- including meaningful culture in every lesson
- reinforcing concepts from other classes in the foreign language class
- using authentic songs, games, stories and rhymes
- incorporating reading and writing skills
- planning varied lessons that appeal to differing interests and learning styles
- providing the students with opportunities to talk about things that are meaningful to them
- assessing students' progress on a regular basis, using a variety of methods
- maintaining open communication about the program and about learner progress with parents, fellow teachers, school and system administrators, and the general public

Rationale

Fluency in a foreign language is a basic life skill that Georgia children need in order to compete in the global marketplace. Four out of five jobs created in the United States are created from foreign trade. The United States needs citizens who can speak another language in order to maintain our national security and our economic competitiveness.

In addition, foreign language study has consistently been shown to increase students' performance in other disciplines, such as math, reading and language arts. Children who have studied a foreign language in elementary school achieve expected gains and score higher on standardized tests of reading, language arts and math than children who have not studied a foreign language. For a summary of current research and an annotated bibliography of research on the positive effects of early language learning, please contact Elizabeth Webb at the Georgia Department of Education: (404) 651-7275, or *ewebb@doe.k12.ga.us*.

Results

When the Georgia Department of Education looked at Iowa Test of Basic Skills scores for the spring of 2000, staff members found that students enrolled in the ESFL model program scored higher than the state average on each of the six sub-tests. This corroborates evidence gathered by Dr. Carol Saunders of Georgia State University. In her dissertation, Dr. Saunders compared a group of third grade students who had been enrolled in the ESFL Model program with a group of students from the same school who were one year older and had not been enrolled in the program. She found that the group that had studied foreign language scored significantly higher in Math than the group that had not had the benefit of the program. They also scored higher in reading, but the difference was not considered statistically significant.

In addition, program assessments conducted by the Center for Applied Linguistics (CAL) attest to the fact that students do make good progress learning the second language. In 1997 and in 1998, CAL conducted interviews with a random sample of students enrolled in the program and reached the following conclusions:

> The evidence that is available seems to indicate that the students in the Georgia ESFL Model Program are making impressive progress toward mastering foreign languages.
>
> A substantial percentage of students in the ESFL Model Program exceeded expectations in their ability to comprehend and speak the languages they are learning.

In 2001, yet another CAL study was commissioned. This study involved videotaped interviews of a random sample of Kindergarten, third and fifth grade students who had been in the program. The Early Language Learning Listening and Oral Proficiency Assessment (ELLOPA) and the Student Oral Proficiency Assessment (SOPA) were used to determine students' level of proficiency in oral fluency, grammar, vocabulary and listening comprehension. The results were compared to see if students were making steady gains in performance over the years. The study again confirmed that students in the Georgia ESFL Model Program were making commendable progress in learning a second language, with fifth graders approaching the intermediate level of proficiency. The 2001 CAL study concluded:

> These results are higher than any known average ELLOPA/SOPA ratings in other foreign language elementary programs in the United States.... The ESFL Model Program is a true model program, not just for Georgia, but also for the country.

Visiting an ESFL Model Program

The Georgia ESFL Model School programs serve as important resources for other schools interested in developing their own early language program. Each model program serves as a demonstration site and cordially welcomes visitors throughout the school year. Model program teachers also serve as leaders in the area of foreign language in the elementary school, regularly presenting at state, regional and national conferences.

For information on visiting one of our model programs, contact Elizabeth Webb at the Georgia Department of Education: (404) 651-7275, *ewebb@doe.k12.ga.us*

Participating Schools

Most model program sites receive approximately half of their funding from the Georgia Department of Education, through an annual appropriation of the Georgia General Assembly.

The remainder of the cost of the program is financed by the local school district.

*Denotes model program funded 100% by the local school district.

Atlanta Public Schools
E. Rivers Elementary, French*
Morris Brandon Elementary, French*
Fickett Elementary, French
Centennial Park Elementary, Spanish

Catoosa County
Graysville Elementary, Spanish

Cherokee County
Little River Elementary, Spanish

Canton Elementary, Spanish

Columbia County
South Columbia Elementary, Spanish
Stevens Creek Elementary, Spanish

Decatur City Schools
Clairemont Elementary, Spanish*
College Heights Elementary, Spanish*
Oakhurst Elementary, Spanish
Glenwood Elementary, Spanish*
Westchester Elementary, Spanish
Winnona Park Elementary, Spanish*

DeKalb County
Austin Elementary, German
Rowland Elementary, German

Dougherty County
Lake Park Elementary, Spanish
Sherwood Elementary, Spanish

Douglas County
Lithia Springs Elementary, French
Chapel Hill Elementary, French
Holly Springs Elementary School, French

Forsyth County
Big Creek Elementary, French
Chestatee Elementary, Spanish

Fulton County
Mimosa Elementary, Japanese

Gwinnett County
Rockbridge Elementary, Spanish

Richmond County
Lake Forest Hills Elementary, Spanish

Sumter County
Sumter County Primary, Spanish
Sumter County Elementary, Spanish
Cherokee Elementary, Spanish

Taliaferro County
Taliaferro County Elementary, Spanish

Whitfield County
Varnell Elementary School, Spanish

Printed in the United States
41563LVS00002B/92